You Are Anointed With Power!

Tim and Kim Grant

T K Ministries

7 Stonebridge Way
Kirkby
Liverpool
L32 1DA

www.tkministries.org

Copyright © Tim and Kim Grant 2021

The right of Tim and Kim Grant to be identified as the authors of this work has been asserted by the authors in accordance with the Copyright, Designs and Patents Act 1988.

All rights reserved.

No part of this publication may be reproduced or transmitted in any form or by any means, electronic or mechanical, including photocopy, recording or any information storage and retrieval system, without permission in writing from the authors or publisher.

Printed in the UK.

ISBN:	978-1-80049-443-5
Typeface:	Sabon Next LT
Graphic design:	Thirteen Creative

Unless otherwise indicated, Scripture quotations are taken from THE HOLY BIBLE, NEW INTERNATIONAL VERSION®,

NIV® Copyright © 1973, 1978, 1984, 2010 by Biblica, Inc.™ Used by permission. All rights reserved worldwide.

Scripture quotations marked (NASB) are taken from the NEW AMERICAN STANDARD BIBLE Copyright © 1960, 1963, 1963, 1968, 1971, 1972, 1973, 1975, 1979, 1995 by Lockman Foundation.

Scripture quotations marked (MSG) are taken from THE MESSAGE. Copyright © by Eugene H. Peterson 1993, 1994, 1995, 1996, 2000, 2001, 2002. Used by permission of NavPress. All rights reserved. Represented by Tyndale House Publishers, Inc.

Scripture quotations marked (TPT) are from The Passion Translation®. Copyright © 2017, 2018 by Passion & Fire Ministries, Inc. Used by permission. All rights reserved. ThePassionTranslation.com.

Disclaimer: The events in this book are written from the perspective of the authors and how they remember them. They have sought to present a factual account.

To contact the authors:
Please send an email to: admin@tkministries.org
More information can be found online: www.tkministries.org

Endorsements

'Easy to read and a comprehensive discipleship resource. Not only a book on moving in the power of the Holy Spirit, but a holistic guide to being a covenant-living people of a covenant-keeping God. Testimonies, historical facts, personal examples to challenge, convict and convince of how we are able to live in the fullness of life that Christ promised, with signs and wonders following'.

Christine Larkin Restoration House

'I have known Tim and Kim for many years and have deeply respected their personal, intimate walk with the Lord. From being a local pastor to that of his current ministry as an evangelist, Tim has always shown a deep passion to follow after God and to learn the ways of the Holy Spirit.

If you want to know God in a richer more fulfilling way then this book will have many golden truths explained to you, the reader, which you may incorporate into your own walk. Prepare to be blessed as well as deeply challenged by their total commitment to this lifestyle.

You will both laugh and be in awe as Tim and Kim and the Holy Spirit take you on an adventure in faith that will create a deep longing in your spirit. Before entering the ministry, Tim was a plumber and the similarities of his walk with God and

Endorsements

the miracles he has witnessed would be worthy, in my opinion, of comparison to a modern day Smith Wigglesworth.

You will be richly blessed by going on a journey with Tim and Kim and the Holy Spirit through the pages of this book.'

Ian Andrews Citadel Ministries

'During the relatively short time that Julie and I have known Tim and Kim they have become good friends. We love and trust them and it is such a joy and blessing that they have moved home to Liverpool. As we have talked, laughed and fellowshipped together it has become clear to us that Tim and Kim are the 'real deal'.

Like ourselves they have been in ministry for a while now! God has used them both locally and internationally. They are relational people and as they share their story you clearly hear the message of God's faithfulness to them on their journey over and over again. They openly share their experience which is filled with Father's grace and goodness.

Tim and Kim freely minister in their God given anointing. Their words are filled with a focus on Father and His goodness that inspires faith and hope to rise in the hearts of those who hear them. They minister in both humility and great confidence.

The question we have to ask ourselves is, "Am I allowing the Holy Spirit to lead my life as a vessel He can use?" and if so, "How can I get to the place where the Holy Spirit can release His power through me so that I begin to see breakthrough after breakthrough?"

Through the pages of this book we find the answers and are encouraged and equipped to be 'anointed with power' just as Tim and Kim continue to model faith for healing on a daily basis.'

Dave Connolly Toxteth Tabernacle Church

'Tim and Kim's book is a treasure trove of wisdom, insight and revelation into divine healing. This book is not just another 'how to book' but an example of how God works through His willing and yielded vessels. Testimonies of breakthroughs bring faith to the reader and inspire one to step out with boldness and expectation.

The teaching is accessible and uncomplicated - a real practical guide. I thoroughly recommend this book. I encourage you to read it several times to absorb all the richness of the nutrients contained within it.'

Tim Eldridge Presence Ministries International

Acknowledgements

This book could not have been written without the input of many people over the years. Giants in God who have paid a price to take ground to enable us to step into everything that God intended us to be. There is not enough room here to mention them all but we do feel we should acknowledge a few of them.

Our friend Brenda Southon who spent hours typing, proofreading and correcting this manuscript and without whose time this book would have taken much longer to get into print!

Mike Pusey and Derek Brown who led the church where we have spent much of our life and ministry. Their desire to release others to step out in the gifts of the Spirit and their encouragement particularly to us to minister to those who are sick in body, mind and spirit started us on our journey to see God's Kingdom manifested in power here on earth. Derek's 'Rapha School' laid a strong Biblical foundation in our lives and I am sure that many of the concepts are included within this book.

Ian Andrews who willingly visited time and again to support a young couple who were planting a church in a small town in North East Hampshire. He taught us how God can move in power through ordinary believers and encouraged us over the years to follow his example by raising up others to follow in healing footsteps.

Bill Johnson who encouraged us through hours of recorded ministry and many amazing testimonies. Bill was humble and approachable enough to spend time talking with me in an airport departure lounge and invited Kim and myself to see behind the scenes at Bethel Church.

For the writings of Smith Wigglesworth, the great apostle of faith and a man from a similar background to my own, for his passion and example of how we can uncompromisingly put our trust in God's Word. He demonstrated that we can step out in faith and see God move in power. The amazing testimonies that we have recorded are a constant inspiration.

Likewise, Kenneth Hagin, the great minister of faith, who taught us so much about living and moving in faith in God's Word through his books and ministry.

We hope this book adequately reflects their input and we are sure that those familiar with their teaching will see much of it within these pages. *'There is nothing new under the sun'* (Ecclesiastes 1:9) and *'the wise man brings treasure both old and new out of his store house'* (Matthew 13:52) and so I make no apology for doing so! I hope that through our insights we have added positively to their legacy. We pray that this book will help you to step into all that Father God has for you.

Tim Grant

Dedication

To all those fellow followers of our Lord who have a Godly dissatisfaction with where they are and a desire to see more of God at work in power by the Holy Spirit working through them in this world.

For Becky and Tom, our daughter and son, who are God's love gift to us.

For Gareth and Emma, we could not be blessed by finer partners for our children.

For Elijah, Hope, Eden and Reuben, our grandchildren, who are the delight of our hearts.

And for Alfie the dog, not to be left out!

Contents

Endorsements 4
Acknowledgements 7
Dedication 9
Contents 10
Prologue 11
Heightening Our Expectations 14
Healing in the Old Testament 35
Healing in the New Testament 52
The Roots of Sickness 75
Understanding Authority 99
Living by Faith 118
The Name of Jesus part 1 146
The Name of Jesus part 2 155
Dealing with Disappointment 176
Hindrances to Healing 183
Full of the Holy Spirit 206
Guidelines for Ministry 218
Personal Testimony of Healing 224
Recommended by the Author 232

Prologue

I gave my life to Christ in my late teens after several years of tearing around the countryside as part of a motorcycle gang. The realisation that there is a supreme being in existence brought me up with a short, sharp shock! As I have always been rather an 'all or nothing' kind of character I quickly concluded that this revelation of Jesus required me to give myself wholeheartedly to the truth of the gospels and seek to implement it in totality into my way of living.

Throughout my walk with God I have been motivated to believe for more, reach for more and see His Holy Spirit accomplish more. He is El Shaddai, the All Sufficient One. He is the God of not just enough but more than enough!

From the early days of my journey I have been provoked to see men and women everywhere live in the fullness of all that Christ's sacrifice has purchased for us. My spirit is constantly offended by the suffering of His children especially in the area of sickness and disease. Jesus has done everything necessary to defeat the work of the enemy and we are to seek to bring healing and wholeness to a fallen world. *'And He said to them, "As you go into all the world, preach openly the wonderful news of the gospel to the entire human race! Whoever believes the good news and is baptized will be saved.... And these miracle signs will accompany* those who believe: They will drive out demons in My Name.... And they will lay hands on the sick and heal them"' (Mark 16:15-18 TPT).

I have sought to put into practice the teaching and example of our Lord Jesus and the writers of the New Testament. The many miraculous exploits of healing and deliverance we have recorded throughout Scripture are both my tutor and inspiration. I am indebted to those saints who have gone before who leave us with such a rich legacy of determination to see the working of the Holy Spirit. I owe a debt of gratitude to those who walk with me in this age who are companions and fellow workers for the Kingdom.

I am challenged by Jesus' words, *'I tell you this timeless truth: The person who follows Me in faith, believing in Me, will do the same mighty miracles that I do – even greater miracles than these because I go to be with My Father! For I will do whatever you ask Me to do when you ask in My Name. And that is how the Son will show what the Father is really like and bring glory to Him. Ask Me anything in My Name and I will do it for you!'* (John 14:12-14 TPT). This is a mandate given to all disciples down through the ages and one that I am looking to see fulfilled in my life.

Throughout the chapters of this book I have shared some of the lessons we have learned over the past forty years of ministry. I have included testimonies of miracles and healings that I have been privileged by His grace to witness. There have been disappointments along the way and I hope that we have managed to glean some insight from such experiences, ever mindful of the fact that there is no lack in our Father God. He is faithful to His Word that declares, *'by His (Jesus') wounds we are healed'* (Isaiah 53:5).

My hope is that in the following pages the reader will be encouraged and stirred to aspire to be the people of God that this world desperately needs us to be. A people anointed with the power of the Holy Spirit from on high (Acts 1:8) who are carriers of the life changing message of love and provision from a Father reaching out to His children.

'Never doubt God's mighty power to work in you and accomplish all this. He will achieve infinitely more than your greatest request, your most unbelievable dream, and exceed your wildest imagination! He will outdo them all, for His miraculous power constantly energises you' (Ephesians 3:20 TPT).

Let us be such a people!

Tim Grant
March 2021

CHAPTER ONE

Heightening Our Expectations

Ever since the day I submitted my life to the Lordship of Christ Jesus I have been convinced that the church is intended to be a people who are 'anointed with power'. I do not believe that you can read the New Testament without coming to that same conclusion. If we take a look at Luke 24:49 we read that Jesus told the disciples to *'stay in the city until you have been clothed with power from on high'*. Just as the early disciples were commanded to operate in power so must we function in the same way in the twenty first century.

'Jesus said to them, "go into all the world and preach the gospel to all creation. He who has believed and has been baptized shall be saved. But he who has disbelieved shall be condemned. And these signs will accompany those who have believed: in My Name they will cast out demons, they will speak with new tongues, they will pick up serpents and if they drink any deadly poison it will not hurt them.

They will lay their hands on the sick and they will recover". So then when the Lord Jesus had spoken to them He was received up into heaven and sat down at the right hand of God. And they went out and preached everywhere while the Lord worked with them and confirmed the Word by the signs that followed' (Mark 16:15-20 NAS).

Let us see what we can learn from this Scripture. Firstly, Jesus declared that *'these signs will follow those who believe'* intimating that you will know those who are believers because this is what will be happening around them. Do you agree that this is a fair interpretation? If it is indeed a logical analysis of this verse then the flip side is also rational; that we will know those who do not believe because such signs will not be evident in their lives. The onus is on us to ensure that these signs happen in our ministry to demonstrate our faith in God. In line with verse 20, when we declare what Jesus has promised we can be confident that He will turn up and do exactly what He said He would do! If we become 'believing believers' then we will speak the words that Jesus spoke and we will see and minister the very healings that Jesus intends for us to accomplish.

This may sound rather presumptuous but remember that Jesus said, *'if anyone steadfastly believes in Me, he will himself be able to do the things that I do; and he will do even greater things than these, because I go to the Father'* (John 14:12 AMP). I know this to be true in my own life because in recent years as I have sought to 'do those things that Jesus did' I have discovered that God intervenes and honours His Word. It is not just theory; it has become our experience. It is both exciting and thrilling! For the first few years of my Christian walk I was passionate and then slowly I drifted into what I can only describe as a state of mediocrity. Just going through the actions, seeking to believe the verses above but never really seeing that much fruit. Then Father God got hold of me in a new way and everything changed and I have to tell you that I do not want to go back! I am no longer satisfied with my previous experience.

This phrase in Mark 16:17 is absolute; *'these signs will accompany those who have believed'*. Signs are expected to follow believers. It has often been said that "the trouble with the modern churches is that the believers are following signs rather than signs following the believers". Some will travel vast distances to various destinations around the world where they hear reports of miracles taking place rather than believing that those very same expressions of the Holy Spirit's power can happen at their own hands.

Let us visit the well-known account in 2 Kings 4 where the wife of a man who was part of a company of prophets came to Elisha to ask for help. Her husband had just died and she had fallen into debt and was about to lose her sons into slavery to settle those arrears. It is at this point that she came to Elisha to ask for his assistance and he asks her, *'what shall I do for you? Tell me, what do you have in your house?'* The woman replies, *'your maidservant has nothing in the house except a jar of oil'* (2 Kings 4:2 AMP).

I would like to pose two questions which are comparable to those that Elisha had asked of this woman. Firstly, what are you expecting from God? I believe there is a direct correlation between what our expectations of God are and the measure that we receive from Him. In recent years Father has been challenging me and I believe that He is provoking all of His people to believe for more. Our local church entered 2004 with the expression 'more in 2004' and something in my spirit responded, "Father God, I want more! I am fed up with what I have. Father, if You want us to have more then that is what I am going to have this year!" God continues to challenge us to believe Him for abundance. It is an ongoing encounter.

That year we felt led to purchase a tent that seats 1,300 people costing £25,000 which I did not have in my bank account. We previously had owned a tent which seated 350 people and God told me to give it away to a church in Sri Lanka. We did just that and arranged to ship the marquee out to the island even though we did not actually have the money to pay for its passage. On the morning that I was transporting the canvas to the docks the postman delivered an envelope and on opening the letter I found that it contained a cheque from a church that I had worked with previously. An accompanying note read; 'heard you are sending your tent to Sri Lanka. We would like to give you something towards the cost'. The cheque was for the amount of £250. I had no idea how much it would cost to ship the tent and so I duly arrived at the docks and waited for the guy in charge of costings to calculate the price of the passage. I was delighted when he announced the bill was £230. Praise God! On the way home, I asked Father, "why was the cheque for £250?" to which He replied, "it cost you £20 in petrol to get here". God is so good and takes care of every detail!

Consequently, we found ourselves in the position of no longer having a tent but with five upcoming 'tent events' booked. I began to receive phone calls from pastors saying, "Tim, we understand that you've sold your tent. What about our event?" I told them that I had actually given the tent away. Understandably, they were anxious as they had spent thousands of pounds organising their events and now were asking, "what's going to happen?" I replied that, "God is going to work it out" and their overwhelming reaction was, "well, He had better!"

We prayed and God directed us to source and buy another marquee and so we stretched our faith as far as we were able and purchased the aforementioned 1,300-seater tent. The day after I had placed the order I received Reinhardt Bonnke's newsletter celebrating ten years of working in Africa. I opened it up and it showed the great evangelist's original tent with the caption

Heightening Our Expectations

'Reinhardt's first tent held 35,000 people'. As I studied the picture, Father said, "See son, you're not thinking big enough!" It had taken every ounce of our faith to believe that God would supply the £25,000, which I want to tell you He did before the tent even arrived in the country. The funds just came in even though we had not announced our need. Cheques just started arriving, praise God!

Father wants us to increase our expectations and let me repeat, I am convinced that there is a direct link between what our expectations of Father are and what we will receive from God.

If we are to see all that He has planned for us then we need to make sure that our expectations of Him come into line with His desires for us. If we read on in this story in 2 Kings 4 we see that the surplus left to the widow once she had sold the oil to discharge her debts was to provide for her and her family's future. Her expectations dictated just how well she would live as the prophet had said to her, *'bring vessels, not a few. Go to the neighbours, your friends, borrow as many pots as you can'*. How expansive is your expectation of God?

The Holy Spirit is not given just so that we might speak in tongues, precious though that is. Rather, He comes that we might be anointed with power. That we might preach the good news with demonstrations of power and go into all the world and declare that the Kingdom of God is at hand; *'heal the sick, raise the dead, cleanse those who have leprosy, drive out demons. Freely you have received, freely give'* (Matthew 10:8).

We have a gospel message that is intended to be a missive of power. When we carry such a message so full of authority then we will begin to see situations and lives radically changed. We experienced just such an occurrence during a healing meeting where a lady had come along to report what had happened to her. We had previously prayed over a handkerchief (in line with Acts 19:12) and sent the cloth to her as she was suffering from a brain tumour.

The consultant had told her that the tumour was inoperable and that she only had a short time to live. She reached out to us for help. Now here was the lady herself telling us of her experience. When she had attended her next scheduled appointment the doctor had greeted her with, "you're looking well! I really didn't expect to see you here today". To which she replied, "after what you said last time I didn't expect to be here today either!"

On hearing that she felt fine the doctor suggested that they carry out a further scan as a matter of urgency to find out the current state of the tumour. The result showed that against all the odds the fast-growing tumour had shrunk back dramatically and now could be considered as operable. The lady was admitted to hospital immediately and underwent an operation that successfully removed the cancerous growth.

On her recovery from the surgery her oncologist advised her that they had best carry out further scans of her whole body. The type of cancer in her brain was known to seed itself in other areas but because she had been considered terminal they had looked no further. The subsequent scan revealed tumours in her lungs. This news had brought her to our healing meeting.

She was scheduled for a further scan that coming week targeting her lungs to help the doctors identify what course of treatment might be most effective. This lady had come to receive prayer for this new problem. As we were ministering to her with our hands on her shoulders, God asked me, "What are you doing?" I replied, "I'm praying, Lord. You are interrupting me, why?"

Father declared that, "In My Kingdom there is a new pair of lungs for this lady". Great!

He directed, "Close your eyes". I did so and immediately in my imagination I saw a video playing of a pair of lungs suspended in space that were inflating and deflating. Father God instructed me; "Give them to her".

"But they're in my head, Lord!" I protested. "How do I get them out?" Father reminded me, "My Kingdom is at hand (Mark 1:15) and in My Kingdom there is a new pair of lungs. You have just seen them. Reach out, take them and give them to her".

I looked the woman in the eyes and I told her, "God's told me to give you a new pair of lungs". She was not a believer and looked at me as if I were a crackpot. However as she had received the handkerchief and seen the power of God work through it, faith was stirring. I reached out into thin air and explained, "God has said that His Kingdom is so near that I am going to reach out and here they are, have them!"

A few days later she duly attended for her scan and I received her phone call. "I have just been for my scan and they looked at my lungs and the consultant's words were, 'this is very strange; it looks like you have a completely new pair of lungs, there is no cancer there'". She went on to explain, "I remembered what you said and I know that God has healed me". She invited me to come to her home as she had gathered ten friends who were all suffering from various cancers. They wanted us to minister to them. Evangelism is easy when we are moving in power!

So I want to repeat the question; "What are you expecting from God?"

I believe that the second question is just as crucial to our understanding and moving in the power of God. Father is asking, "What do you have?" The same question that Elisha asked of the widow. It is only as we understand what we have in God that we can fully minister in the fullness of all that He has won for us.

In Acts 3:1-9 (NAS) we read;

'Now Peter and John were going up to the temple at the ninth hour, the hour of prayer and a certain man who had been lame from his mother's womb was being carried along whom they used to set down every day at the gate of the temple, which is called Beautiful in order to beg money from those who were entering the temple. When he saw Peter and John about to go into the temple he began asking them for money but Peter, along with John, fixed his gaze on him and said, "look at us" and he began to give them his attention expecting to receive something from them. But Peter said "I do not possess silver and gold but what I do have I give to you. In the Name of Jesus Christ the Nazarene walk". And seizing him by the right hand he raised him up and immediately his feet and ankles were strengthened. With a leap he stood upright and began to walk and he entered the temple with them walking and leaping and praising God. And all the people saw him walking and praising God'.

Did you notice what Peter said to the lame man? *'What I do have I give to you'*. Peter understood something of the nature of what he had received from the Lord. There was no room for doubt in him. He seized the man by the right hand and raised him up and we are told that immediately the man's limbs were made stronger. Peter was aware of the anointing on his life and ministered out of confidence in that realisation.

It is my hope that as you read through this book that you will grow in your understanding of what we have been given and that assurance will enable you to minister in greater certainty and power.

I have this vision of the Holy Spirit living in us but He is trapped in a cage which leads to Him being incredibly frustrated! The Holy Spirit that lives in us is the Spirit of God, the Spirit Who was there in Genesis, Who was waiting on God's Word and when God spoke He partnered with Father to see the universe and everything within it come into being. It is the same Spirit Who was ready to resurrect Christ from the dead and this Spirit has been given to us. If we are filled with the Holy Spirit then He wants to break out and fulfil all that He is intent on accomplishing. He wishes to create in us the men and women Father God means us to be. What you are expecting God to do for you and what you believe He has entrusted to you will have a tremendous impact on what you can achieve in His Name.

We can see how these principles worked negatively in the ten spies who were sent to survey the Promised Land. On their return they gave their report; *"we went into the land to which you sent us and it does flow with milk and honey! Here is its fruit. But the people who live there are powerful and the cities are fortified and very large. We saw the descendants of Anak there. The Amalekites live in the Negev, the Hittites, the Jebusites and the Amorites live in the hill country and the Canaanites live near the sea and along the Jordan"*.

Then Caleb silenced the people before Moses and said, "We should go up and take possession of this land for we can certainly do it". But the men who had gone up with him said, "We can't attack those people; they are stronger than we are". And they spread among the Israelites a bad report about the land they had explored' (Numbers 13:27-32).

They continued, *'the land we explored devours those living in it. All the people we saw there are of great size. We saw the Nephilim there, (the descendants of Anak come from the Nephilim). We seemed like grasshoppers in our own eyes and we looked the same to them'* (Numbers 13:32-33).

These spies knew that God had declared that He had given this land to their people. Even though they had seen all that God had done to facilitate their escape from Egypt; He had brought the plagues and He had made a way through the Red Sea. They had witnessed all His miraculous interventions which had brought them to the border of the Promised Land. A land that was exactly as God had said it would be. The Children of God failed to enter in because their expectations of Yahweh were not great enough to lift them above the giants. When our expectancy of God is low then the problems before us can become overwhelming. We find ourselves unable to receive and minister in the fullness of all that Father has given us. Yet our experience of all that He has already done in our lives should be a springboard to all that He wants us to see in the future. If we allow the giants to overwhelm us then we are in danger of being a people who only see the giants of obstacles before us rather than being the giants of faith that God intends us to be.

We are told that they became *'like grasshoppers'* in their own sight and so that was how they were perceived by the inhabitants of the land. We actually have no record that anyone in the land saw the spies or made any comment to them about their stature! Israel's perception of themselves determined the way in which they believed other people viewed them.

I expect the spies thought that they were bringing a balanced account. However God described their feedback as an *'evil report'* (Numbers 13:32 AMP) because they majored on the problem rather than Father's ability to overcome. If we only focus on the difficulties rather than the greatness of our God then we will end up in unbelief and miss out on all the promises that He has for us. Let us get caught up with the awesomeness of God all over again!

When our children were growing up, we were very privileged to live on the edge of town where there were not so many streetlights. Our home backed onto a golf course where I would walk the dog last thing on a summer's night. I would lay on the grass and look up at the stars. I would talk to God, the God Who created this amazing panorama. Who is beyond all this wonder, Who is bigger than everything that I could see or perceive, Who is zooming right in on this planet in a small corner of the Universe, is zooming right in on the nation of England. Is zooming right in on the village of Whitehill and the golf course at the back of my house and was talking to me. I cannot help but think, 'Wow!' This is the God that we serve and this is the God that put His Spirit in us! We need to raise the bar of our expectations. Father wants and is capable of doing so much more that we can imagine.

So, how are we to raise our expectations?

I want us to consider the character of God. I think that as we come to understand the character of a person so it builds our confidence in them. Here are a number of verses which reveal the attributes of God. They speak of aspects of Father voiced by a people who knew their God.

2 Kings 13:23 tells us, *'the Lord was gracious to them and had compassion and showed concern for them because of His covenant with Abraham, Isaac and Jacob. To this day He has been unwilling to destroy them or banish them from His presence'.*

I looked up the meaning of some of these words in the Oxford English Dictionary.

- 'Gracious' ~ kind and courteous. We serve a God Who is caring and considerate. We may not often find much courtesy in our world but we serve a God Who epitomises these virtues.

- 'Compassionate' ~ merciful, giving undeserved favour. Father does not give us what we deserve but rather unmerited preference. He shows an interest in our wellbeing, how we act and the way that we live.

'Who among the gods is like You, O Lord? Who is like You? Majestic in holiness, awesome in glory, working wonders' (Exodus 15:11).

- 'Majestic' ~ having supreme power. Father is above all others. There is no authority that is above Him, He is pre-eminent.

- 'Awesome' ~ inspiring. Our relationship with God should motivate us to cooperate with Him as He performs miracles and remarkable exploits.

'For You are great and do marvellous deeds; You alone are God' (Psalm 86:10).

That position is up for grabs in our society at the moment. There are many people who contend that, "there is this god, there is that god". No, Scripture plainly states; *'You alone are God'*. We need to hold onto that single fact because that very truth is being challenged in our nation more than ever before. There is only one God and He is not the god of other faiths; these other faiths are entirely incompatible with our heavenly Father God.

- 'Great' ~ Our God is unsurpassed by anything else.

- 'Marvellous' ~ Father performs amazing, wonderful feats. This is exactly what our God wants to do among us.

'I will proclaim the Name of the Lord, Oh praise the greatness of our God! He is the Rock, His works are perfect and all His ways are just. A faithful God Who does no wrong, upright and just is He' (Deuteronomy 32:3-4).

- 'The Rock' ~ If our lives are built on God then while everything that surrounds us may be shaken, we will stand firm. When everything else is falling down we will be recognised by the fact that we are kept safe because we are founded on the Rock (Matthew 7:24-27).

- 'His works are perfect' ~ I have learnt not to question this characteristic of Father God. Possibly because I find that banging my head against a brick wall is uncomfortable and so I am trying not to do it any longer! I refrain from questioning His ways and accept that all of His ways are fair. In times past I have queried His intentions. I now fully accept in my heart that He is truly dependable and a God Who does not harm but seeks to prosper us (Jeremiah 29:11). We need to settle these truths in our hearts.

'The Lord is slow to anger, abounding in love and forgiving sin and rebellion' (Numbers 14:18).

Father God is not waiting for us with a big stick rather the Word states that He is not quick to wrath. This was brought home to me when as a young father I was helping my daughter to learn to walk. We were typical proud parents and I was holding my little girl and encouraging her to "walk to Mummy" who was standing a few feet away. Becky stepped forward with a big smile and then, of course, she falls down. I rush across, pick her up and give her a big cuddle.

I clearly heard Father God ask me, "are you going to smack her?" which drew the shocked reply, "what sort of father do you think I am?" God answered; "that is the sort of father you think I am. I know, just as you do, that one day your daughter will walk, she'll run, she'll jump, she'll skip and do all those things that she hasn't done yet. Just as I know that one day you will walk, you will run, jump, leap and do all the things you are meant to do in your journey with Me. When you fall over I am not waiting with a big stick. I am waiting with loving arms to pick you up and set you up to have another go!"

We serve a God Who is *'slow to anger'* and Who is overflowing in love towards His children. He forgives our wrongdoing and disobedience. Not just our missteps but also our wilful wrongdoing.

As we meditate on such verses we begin to comprehend Who this God is that we serve and the nature of His heart towards us. We do well to remind ourselves often of His temperament and His wonderful characteristics. Let us take a look at what God says about Himself with reference to healing;

'If you listen carefully to the voice of the Lord your God and do what is right in His eyes, if you pay attention to His commands and keep all His decrees, I will not bring on you any of the diseases which I brought on the Egyptians, for I am the Lord Who heals you' (Exodus 15:26).

- He declares Himself to be the God Who heals us.

'Worship the Lord your God and His blessing will be on your food and water. I will take away sickness from among you' (Exodus 23:25).

- He declares that He is the Lord Who removes illness from us.

'Blessed is he who has regard for the weak, the Lord delivers him in times of trouble, the Lord will protect him and preserve his life. He will bless him in the land and not surrender him to the desire of his foes. The Lord will sustain him on his sickbed and restore him from his bed of illness' (Psalm 41:1).

When we read passages like this we can begin to appreciate in greater measure the very nature of Father God and His commitment to His people and our wellbeing. Having such an understanding will help us to realise what He is like, what His desires are for our lives and it will help us to expect great things from Him. I want to encourage you in this realisation, as God has encouraged me, to expect great things from God and be prepared to do great things for God!

This is the motto we have made our own; 'we are expecting great things from God, we are going to do great things for God!' Especially in the area of healing.

We are working towards having such a mind-set that where sickness or even death is concerned we are completely sure of God's intent to move in power and intervene in any given situation.

This is somewhat of a quest for us; to develop that mind-set, a change in our consciousness.

As has been said above, it is important that we appreciate the depths of the character of Father God and His compassion and His concern for His people. We need to recognise afresh His majesty, the fact that He rules, that He is the Rock on which we build our lives. He is our salvation, our comfort, our inheritance, our strength and our song. Everything within Father's heart is directed towards our blessing and it is really important that we get hold of that truth.

The healing of disease and sickness can be seen in this overall context of restoration and provision and part of God's unchanging nature to bless us. That is why Paul wrote to the Ephesians (1:17) that he *'keeps asking that the God of our Lord Jesus Christ, the glorious Father may give you the Spirit of wisdom and revelation so that you may know Him better'* and that is why the apostle says to the Colossians (1:9) that he had *'not stopped praying for you to grow in the knowledge of God'*, or as the Living Bible reads, *'that you don't stop learning to know God better and better!'* The Bible is entirely geared up to revealing to us Father God's nature that we might fully understand all aspects of His character.

When God revealed His name to Moses in the burning bush, *'I AM WHO I AM'* (Exodus 3:14), He was conveying something of His make-up. When we read in Exodus 34:5 that God proclaimed the *'Name of the Lord'*, He went on to describe His character and it is important that we take on board all those aspects of Father's identity and the role that He promises to fulfil in the lives of His people.

Our Spirit is to assimilate all that He is from Jehovah Jireh, 'the Lord our provider' to Jehovah Rapha, 'the Lord that heals'.

In the following chapters we will examine the healing aspect of Father's persona and how that was worked out in both the Old and New Testaments.

CHAPTER TWO

Healing in the Old Testament

From the moment that Adam and Eve fell into sin (Genesis 3) death and decay entered the human experience.

Romans 5:12 tells us that, *'just as sin entered the world through one man (Adam) and death through sin, and in this way death came to all men...'*

Sickness is part of the consequence of that original rebellion against God. Father in all of His graciousness and love for His children sought to remedy this situation both before the incarnation of Jesus and since His Son's death and resurrection.

In Genesis 20 we see the first recorded supernatural healing take place when ninety years old *Sarah 'received physical power to conceive a child even when she was long past the age for it ...'* (Hebrews 11:11 AMP).

In Exodus we find the Children of God being delivered from the ten plagues that afflicted Pharaoh and Egypt (Exodus 7:14-11:10). The Psalmist recorded that *'there was not one feeble person among them'*. God delivered them from sickness and disease (Psalm 105:37 AMP).

Clearly, God's people saw relief from sickness, disease and pestilence and the apostle Paul gives us the explanation. He writes of the Children of God's escape from the land of Egypt and their journey towards the Promised Land; *'therefore I do not want you to be unaware that our fathers were all under the cloud and all passed through the sea ..... and all ate the same spiritual food and all drank the same spiritual drink for they were drinking from a spiritual rock which followed them and the rock was Christ'* (1 Corinthians 10:1-4 NAS). Everything comes through Jesus wherever we are in the construct of time!

The Children of God lived by the tenets of the law. Father promised that, *'if you will give earnest heed to the voice of the Lord your God and do what is right in His sight, give ear to His commandments and keep all His statutes, I will put none of the diseases on you which I have brought on the Egyptians. For I am the Lord your Healer'* (Exodus 15:26 NAS).

This is covenant language. This is the language of the 'I AM', the Jehovah Rapha. The self-existent One who mends us and restores us to the original intended model.

Father goes on to say that, *'you shall serve the Lord your God and He will bless your bread and your water and will remove sickness from your midst. There will be no miscarriage or barrenness in your land. I will fulfil the number of your days'*. Which I take to mean that there is to be no premature death (Exodus 23:25-26 NAS). Psalm 91:16 states, *'with long life will satisfy I him'*.

Clearly if the Children of Israel met the conditions then their obedience would result in health and fruitfulness.

Healing was very much part of the covenant that Father God made with His people. Deuteronomy 7:12-15 reiterates the promises of health, wholeness and blessing in every area of life including freedom from sickness and disease.

Firstly, let us look at some of the types of healing that took place under the Old Covenant, this Mosaic Covenant that declared that disease would be removed and health restored.

All down through the ages the people who have known their God have moved in His power to perform exploits.

Healings are not just a New Testament phenomena. We see them in action throughout the Old Testament and indeed in the two centuries plus since Christ ascended to be with His Father.

It is good in our study of healing to take note of some of the means that God uses to heal. It will help us have a more informed understanding of Father's character and encourage us to seek to step out more in His power. I say 'means' because I do not subscribe to methods. Every miracle that I have read of is different. God moves in infinite variety!

Before we are in a position to exercise faith for healing we need to be aware of what the Scripture teaches and to know the revealed will of God. We can learn from instances in the Bible and incorporate them as weapons in our armoury.

- The first means of healing in the Old Testament we can examine is prayer. In Genesis 20 we read that Abraham prayed to God and God healed Abimelech, his wife and his slave girls so that they could have children again. Now if you remember the account, Abraham was afraid for his life and so had omitted to tell Abimelech that in fact Sarah was his wife and the Lord struck Abimelech's household and they became barren. On discovering Abraham's reticence, Abimelech ordered Abraham to remedy the situation. So Abraham prays and the king's household is healed.

  Again in 1 Kings 13 we see how King Jeroboam had stretched out his hand as he ordered that the man of God before him be seized and when he did so his hand immediately shrivelled up. So the king asked the man of God to remedy the situation. We read that the man of God from Judah interceded with the Lord and the King's hand was restored. The man of God prays and the king is healed.

  Two clear examples of how our prayers are one means that God will use to bring about healing and I am sure that all of us have prayed in this way.

- Healing came through declaring the Word of God. The Psalmist tells us in Psalm 107:19-20 that, *'they cried to the Lord in their trouble and He saved them from their distress. He sent forth His Word and healed them. He rescued them from the grave'*. There is tremendous power in God's Word that we have only just begun to tap into and we need to go deeper.

  God is totally committed to seeing His Word fulfilled. Remember He tells us in Isaiah 55:11, *'so is with My Word that goes out from My mouth: it will not return to Me empty but it will accomplish what I desire and it will achieve the purpose for which I sent it'*. It is good to confess the Word over ourselves. It is good to confess the Word to our friends and into each other's lives and come to a place of agreement with the Scriptures. When I am feeling unwell, the first thing I do is to speak the Word of God over my life rather than reach for the paracetamol. I declare Psalm 91 over myself until my body comes into line with the Scripture. We should develop the habit of taking the medicine of the Word! *'He who dwells in the secret place of the Most High …. no harm will befall you, no plague will come near your tent …. he will call upon Me and I will answer him'* (Psalm 91:1, 10, 15 AMP).

- Healing came through signs and wonders. In 2 Kings 13:20-21 we read that Elisha died and he was buried. In the location where his body was laid to rest it was quite common for Moabite raiding parties to enter that part of country in the spring. During one such foray they came across some Israelites who were burying a man. On spying the approach of the band of raiders the funeral party unceremoniously tossed the corpse into Elisha's tomb to facilitate a quick escape. When the body touched Elisha's bones the man revived and stood up on his feet!

Several years ago we visited Winchester Cathedral and found St. Swithun's shrine there. The Bishop of Winchester died in 862AD. At various times there have been displayed on the walls of the cathedral crutches, walking frames and various kinds of props from pilgrims who had visited St. Swithun's shrine, been healed and left their now redundant aids behind. Legend has it that when St. Swithun died, being quite a humble guy, he stipulated that his body be buried outside the cathedral building. His wish was initially honoured for nine years until the monks decided he really ought to be interred in a more honourable position. So they went to dig him up and the moment the spade touched the ground there was a clap of thunder, the heavens opened and it rained for forty days and nights. Hence we have the adage 'if it rains on St. Swithun's feast day (the fifteenth of July) then it will continue for forty days'. Having been deterred, a hundred years passed until some more persistent monks managed to re-site the remains inside the cathedral itself.

A small tunnel was built to access the bones and called a 'holy hole'. Pilgrims would crawl along this hole and get as close to St. Swithun's remains as they could and they experienced healing. So on the wall of the cathedral their now redundant crutches were hung as a testament. Such was the power displayed there that St. Swithun's shrine was one of the most visited relics in medieval Britain.

Like Elisha's bones, there was a residual anointing that was stored up in Swithun's remains. It would be pretty amazing if we moved so powerfully in the anointing of God that even after we are long gone that people just passing by our grave would get healed! It would certainly come under the category of being a sign and wonder!

Father God just loves to step out of the box and break free of the limits that our minds and experience put upon Him. He is not about formulas and we too are not to be constrained by rigid methods but rather to move in His power as we perceive what Father is saying and doing in each given situation. We are to think outside of the box!

- The fourth aspect we see is the working of miracles. We recognise this as one of the gifts of the Spirit (1

Corinthians 12:10). They did ok in the Old Testament too! In 1 Kings 17:20-23 we read that Elijah *'cried out to the Lord, "O Lord my God have You brought tragedy upon this widow with whom I am staying by causing her son to die?" Then he stretched himself out on the boy three times and cried to the Lord, "O Lord my God, let this boy's life return to him". The Lord heard Elijah's cry and the boy's life was returned to him and he lived. Elijah picked up the child, carried him down from the room in the house, gave him to his mother and said "Look, your son is alive!"'*

Later on in 2 Kings 4:32-37 we read of Elisha, Elijah's student, who was carrying on the good work. He had reached the house of the Shunammite woman and there was her son lying dead on the couch. Elisha went in, shut the door on the two of them and prayed to the Lord. The prophet got on to the bed and laid on the boy, mouth to mouth, eyes to eyes, hands to hands and as he stretched himself out upon him, the boy's body grew warm. Elisha turned away and walked back and forth in the room and again got back on the bed, stretched himself out upon the lad once more and the boy sneezed seven times and opened his eyes!

I have often wondered why the boy sneezed seven times. It is an ancient tradition that when Father God breathed that very first breath into Adam, the initial sign of life was that Adam sneezed. It is just a tradition, there is no Biblical proof but it is a quite lovely snippet. This gives rise to our habit of saying, 'bless you' when somebody sneezes. It is out of respect to that tradition.

These incidences from the lives of the two prophets clearly show that there is a place for the working of miracles. It is more than just praying. Rather it is combining our faith with our prayer and then taking action which brings about healing. We work the miracle.

A more current example comes from a few years ago when we were running a series of healing meetings in Bordon where we lived. A lady came along who did not know Jesus as her Saviour. She was suffering from tunnel vision and described how the condition limited her sight akin to looking through two narrow drinking straws. She could see very little and had no peripheral vision at all. This woman sat half-way back in the hall and she was squinting badly. When we called people forward for prayer, she responded and walked to the front of the meeting.

Father God directed me to spit in her eyes. My text for that evening had been the account from Mark 8:22 where Jesus had spat on a blind man's eyes. Now here was Father telling me to do the same for this lady stood before me. I found myself doing what every man of God has done at least once in his life-time; I chickened out. I found myself wondering, "did I brush my teeth this evening, did we have garlic for dinner?" and with all these thoughts going through my mind I very quickly talked myself out of following Father's instruction. I simply prayed for the woman and sent her back to her seat. The meeting drew to a close and I could see this lady still squinting at me. So fearing God more than the lady, I screwed up my courage to approach her and asked, "You're not healed are you?" to which she replied, "No!"

I admitted, "that's because I didn't do what God told me to do".

The lady pleaded, "I'm desperate! I've been like this for years so whatever He said, please just do it".

"I really think you need to know what Father told me to do!" I insisted and proceeded to tell her exactly how God had directed me.

She cautiously ventured, "If that's what God said then please just do it, I really am desperate!"

If you have ever seen me try to hit a target with any projectile you will quickly have realised that I am severely directionally challenged. Knowing this, I decided to play safe. I spat on my thumbs and rubbed the saliva into the lady's eyes.

Nothing happened. There was no change whatsoever. The woman returned to her seat and we closed the meeting, started to clear the hall and pack up the chairs, PA etc. The building emptied and as we walked into the foyer the caretaker called out, "Can you come into the ladies loo please?"

We followed him into the rest room to see that one of the cubicles had been completely wrecked and we imagined, rightly or wrongly, that this lady in her frustration had probably gone in there and put her foot through the wall. So here was a depressing end to the evening! We returned home somewhat subdued and wondering, "God, what was that all about?"

The following morning the phone rang bright and early which is just what you need when you have been tossing and turning all night, mulling over the previous evening's events. I picked up the receiver to hear the shrieking voice of a hysterical woman. I realised that it was the woman from the previous night's meeting and it crossed my mind that she was phoning to tell me that she intended to sue me! I managed to calm her down and to finally understand what she was trying to communicate. She recounted how when she went to bed the previous evening her vision was as bad as ever with no improvement whatsoever. On waking that morning she discovered that she could see perfectly; her vision had been restored. Praise God!

The working of a miracle. It is a combination of faith and prayer and then taking specific action which brings about the healing.

- There are medical means. 2 Kings 20:7 tells us that Isaiah said, *'prepare a poultice of figs. They did so and applied it to the boil and he recovered'*. Clearly God has enabled man to develop knowledge that allows us to intervene in the body's natural processes and to help those processes complete their work. I am sure that all of us have benefitted from the medical profession at some point in our lives!

- Let us consider the word of knowledge. In 2 Kings 5 3:16 we find the account of Naaman's healing from leprosy;

'And the servant girl said to her mistress, 'if only my master would see the prophet who is in Samaria, he would cure him of his leprosy'. So Naaman went to his master and told him what the girl of Israel had said. 'By all means go' the King of Syria replied, 'and I will send a letter to the King of Israel'. So Naaman left and took with him ten talents of silver, six thousand shekels of gold and ten sets of clothing. The letter he took to the King of Israel read 'with this letter I am sending my servant Naaman to you so that you may cure him of his

leprosy'. And as soon as the King of Israel read the letter he tore his robes and said 'am I God, can I kill and bring back to life? Why does this fellow send someone to me to be cured of leprosy? See how he is trying to pick a quarrel with me'. Now when Elisha, the man of God, heard that the King of Israel had torn his robes, he sent him this message. 'Why have you torn your robes? Make the man come to me and he will know that there is a prophet in Israel'. So Naaman went with his horses and chariots and he stopped at the door of Elisha's house. Elisha sent a messenger out to him to say to him 'go wash yourself seven times in the Jordan and your flesh will be restored and you will be cleansed'. But Naaman went away angry and said 'I thought that he would surely come out to me, that he would stand, that he would call on the name of the Lord his God, that he would wave his hand over the spots and cure me of my leprosy. Are not the Abanah and Pharpar, the rivers of Damascus better than any of these waters of Israel? Couldn't I wash in them and be cleansed?' So he turned and he went off in a rage. Now Naaman's servants went to him and said, 'my father, if the prophet had told you to do some great thing wouldn't you have done it? How much more then when he tells you, wash and be cleansed?' So he went down and he dipped himself in the Jordan seven times, as the man of the God had told him to do and his flesh was restored and he became clean like that of a young boy. Then Naaman and all his attendants went back to the man of God, Elisha, and he stood before him and said, 'now I know that there is no god in all the world except in Israel. Please accept now a gift from your servant'. The prophet answered, 'as surely as the Lord lives Whom I serve, I will not accept a thing' and even though Naaman urged him he continued to refuse'.

There are a number of things we can learn from this account of healing in the Old Testament. First of all: know your gifting. Elisha knew it, the King of Israel did not. Elisha was cool and collected; he knew his anointing. The King of Israel tore his robes and threw a fit because he knew he did not have it. It is important that we are confident in our hearts and that we own our anointing. We recognise that we carry the gift of healing.

Secondly, we need to understand what God is looking to do. As best as possible we need to be able to see the whole picture because Father God did not just want to heal Naaman. He wanted to do so much more in his life. He wanted to prove to him that He is the only God, not just one of many gods with a small 'g'. As far as possible we need to be able to see the whole picture of what Father is wanting to achieve in the life of the sick person.

Thirdly, very importantly, we should be aware that we are not to be under any kind of pressure from other people's expectations. Elisha did not come out and wave his hands and call upon God and do the business as Naaman thought he should. Elisha was not under that kind of pressure. We need to learn that we should not be compelled to pray in a particular style. Just because a particular hero of the faith ministers in a certain way does not mean that Father wants you to operate in the same manner. We are each unique and, more importantly, the person that you are ministering to is unique and so we must be intent on hearing God for each individual person.

Fourthly, we need to be open to Father and hear what He is saying. Elisha knew exactly what to do and how God wanted to heal Naaman. If people come back to you and they appear not to have been healed firstly check that they carried out whatever action you felt God had directed them to do.

There is often a conflict that goes on, especially when it might be something out of the ordinary or simply something they find difficult. Just as Naaman was upset that it was the Jordan that he was told to bathe in. There is a battle being waged in the mind. We need to help people work that through just as Naaman's friends did; they came alongside their master and helped him to come to the place where he was actually willing to carry out what God had told him to do.

We also need to be careful not to use it as an excuse for our deficit of power. The person may well not have done what you told them to do. Or they may have. Sick people do not need beating up; they need building up. We must never say, 'you didn't do what I said'. Rather, we get alongside them, we encourage them and we bolster them up. We must be wary of falling into this trap and using it as an excuse for our lack of faith or discernment that has delayed the healing.

Finally, remember that healing is a free gift from God. If you hear of anybody charging for ministry, it is a big 'No, no'! Elisha would not take a penny, not one talent of silver, not one shekel of gold, not one set of clothing.

So, to recap. In the Old Testament we see that healing came through prayer, the declaration of the Word of God, working of signs and wonders, working of miracles, medical intervention and through the word of knowledge. They are all examples of means of how God healed in the Old Testament and are to be an inspiration as we continue to expect great things from God and step out to do great things for God.

We should always be willing to open ourselves to the leading of the Holy Spirit and be prepared to step outside of the box. Let us be encouraged by the many ways in which Father wishes to work through us.

Let us now look forward to the New Covenant. *'The ministry Jesus has received is as superior to theirs (Levitical priests) as the covenant of which He is Mediator is superior to the old one (Mosaic) and it is founded on better promises'* (Hebrews 8:6).

The Old Covenant promised to make Israel the people of God but did not provide the power necessary for Israel to keep the covenant. They broke the covenant by their disobedience. Under the New Covenant Christ provided the means for covenant to be eternally instituted through the blood of His perfect sacrifice. Christ cleanses our hearts so that we may serve Him in holiness.

'Jesus has become the guarantee of a better covenant' (Hebrews 7:22). We can have complete confidence in the New Covenant. It is based on Jesus, the superior revelation of God and the superior Mediator of God's covenant. As God Who became flesh, Jesus can guarantee forgiveness is available from God for those who trust Him. As the only human Who fulfilled completely the obligations of the Old Covenant, Jesus can guarantee His followers are acceptable to God. As Father God has sworn to accept Jesus as the eternal Priest we can be sure He is presenting our petitions to God and is able to save us. Jesus Christ thus guarantees that the New Covenant in His blood supersedes all other covenants. It is the way to God and all His provisions, including health and wholeness.

CHAPTER THREE

Healing in the New Testament

As we know, the Old Covenant could never completely and permanently erase the stain of sin. *'If the first covenant had been faultless there would be no occasion sought for a second'* (Hebrews 8:7 NAS). The New Covenant is where Father declares that;

- *'I will remember their sins no more'* ~ Hebrews 8:12
- Jesus is the Mediator of the New Covenant which is *'much superior and more excellent'* ~ Hebrews 8:6 AMP

Jeremiah (31:31) foresaw that *'the days are coming, says the Lord, when I will make a new covenant with My people'*, a prophesy fulfilled by Christ's sacrifice.

The Children of Israel lived under the blood covenant of Father God which promised their freedom from sickness. *'If you pay attention to these laws and are careful to obey them then I will keep My covenant of love with you. I will love and bless you. I will bless the fruit of your womb, the crops of your land, the offspring of your livestock. You will be blessed more than any other people. I will keep you free from every disease'* (Deuteronomy 7:12-15).

If you keep the Ten Commandments (Exodus 20), if you obey the 603 additional laws governing moral, civil and religious matters, if you adhere to the letter of these numerous rules and regulations ....

Then this agreement between God and the nation of Israel ratified by the blood of continual sacrifice of animals (Exodus 24:8, Hebrews 9:19-20) and food offerings, commemorated by the weekly Sabbath and dozens of seasonal festivals ....

Then this covenant, this agreement that *'is only a shadow of the good things that are coming, not the reality of them. For this reason it can never, by the same sacrifices repeated endlessly year after year make perfect those who draw near to worship'* (Hebrews 10:1-2) ....

The Old Covenant was never going to work! It was impossible for the people of Israel to keep up their end of the bargain! *'For all have sinned and fall short of the glory of God'* (Romans 3:23). So Father presented Jesus as a sacrifice of atonement through faith in His blood because of His great love for us; *'while we were still sinners, Christ died for us'* (Romans 5:8).

'For this reason Christ is the Mediator of a new covenant that those who were called may receive the promised eternal inheritance -

now that He has died as a ransom to set them free from the sins committed under the first covenant' (Hebrews 9:15).

Once and for all, Jesus' act as the sacrificial Lamb replaced all the ritualistic blood sacrifices of bulls and goats and sheep and birds. His blood released us from the letter of the Law and made us a people of the Spirit; *'He has made us competent as ministers of a new covenant ~ not of the letter but of the Spirit; for the letter kills, but the Spirit gives life'* (2 Corinthians 3:6).

Our ministry is in the Name of Jesus Who gave Himself to establish that new covenant based on forgiveness of sin. Our ministry is not a legalistic call to follow regulations but rather a joyful invitation to let God's Spirit fill and direct our lives.

Father God, in His graciousness, prepared His people through the utterances of the prophets. *'The time is coming when I will make a new covenant. It will not be like the covenant I made with your forefathers when I brought them out of Egypt. Rather I will put My law in your minds and write it on your hearts. I will be your God and you will be My people. I will forgive you and remember your sin no more'* (Jeremiah 31:31).

Because Israel failed to keep their obligations Father prepared the way for a new covenant relationship based on the renewal of their hearts and desires emphasising His aspiration to have a people who would allow Him to be the Master of their lives.

The new covenant contained radical fresh elements. Firstly, it depended on a transformation of the inner heart rather than slavishly attempting to keep a list of rules and regulations.

Now, under this new covenant, all people are invited to know Father God in a personal way. He deals with individuals rather than whole nations. Forgiveness purchased by Jesus' sacrifice does away with the need for the constant ritual of animal sacrifice.

As part and parcel of this wondrous work of atonement, the prophet Isaiah pointed forward to the sacrificial Lamb Jesus and the fact that *'by His wounds we are healed'* (Isaiah 53:5).

The apostle Peter pointed the Gentiles living in lightly populated regions of the Roman Empire back to that momentous time in history when he declared, *'by His wounds you have been healed'* (1 Peter 2:24).

In time, we are on the same side of the Cross as Peter and so can resonate with his assertion that *'by His stripes we are healed'*. It is a done deal!

We, alongside Peter, alongside the apostles, alongside the early church, are *'ministers of that new covenant'* (2 Corinthians 3:6). With all that this entails for *'all the promises of God in Him are yes and amen to the glory of God'* (2 Corinthians 1:20). We find the fulfilment of all the Old Covenant promises in Jesus which includes our healing and wholeness.

We are part of a kingdom whereby Jesus demonstrated Father's love and compassion for His creation by healing them; emotionally, spiritually and physically. Our Lord has commissioned us to do likewise (Mark 16:18).

Strangely, it has often been asserted that healings and miracles were primarily to establish the New Testament church and were buried in the sands of time with the passing of those first disciples. I want to tell you categorically that I do not believe this in any way, shape or form. I believe that we are called to be a people of power for today!

All through church history there are accounts of healings and miracles and Father God continues to be committed to seeing His Word fulfilled. He is looking for a people who are dedicated to working in partnership with His Holy Spirit to achieve exactly that goal.

F F. Bosworth was a healing revivalist in the early 1900's who ministered mainly in the States and Canada and then latterly in Africa. Here is a quote from his book 'Christ the Healer';

'God seems to be systematically working towards a return to New Testament faith and simplicity. Fundamental Christianity has suffered great damage through the efforts of some to excuse their own spiritual impotence by relegating everything supernatural. Yet deep within the hearts of sincere men (and women) there is a longing to rescue the Book of Acts from becoming nothing more than a historical record and put it back in its proper place for the modern church whereby God can continue to confirm His Word and give proof of the resurrection of His Son in these days.'

I have that longing to see God confirm His Word and to see the signs following. I trust that you do too!

We have taken our whistle stop tour of the Old Testament in the previous chapter and now let us open the New Testament and examine some accounts of healings found there. We are going to again look at the variety of means that God uses to heal. Firstly, of course, let us consider Jesus' life and ministry.

Jesus at times sensed that there was power available to heal all the people in front of Him and we see that demonstrated when after healing Simon's mother-in-law we read that, *'as the sun was setting the people brought to Jesus all who had various kinds of sickness and laying His hands on each one He healed them'* (Luke 4:38-40).

Conversely, let us consider the instance in Jesus' life when He was found at the pool of Bethesda around which was gathered a multitude of sick people. There was one man that God singled out and Jesus healed him. Yet we see in John 5:2-13 that there was a great number of disabled people, *'the blind, the lame, the paralysed'* and I imagine Jesus may well have had to step over them to get to the man He was focused on.

Jesus was led by the Spirit and we who are *'sons of God'* (Romans 8:14) are also to be led by that same Spirit. Jesus knew that He could not do anything outside of the Father (John 5:19). He could only do what He saw the Father doing and indeed He has asked the Father to send us that same Spirit to be our Helper (John 14:16) so that we in turn can see what He is doing. Father wishes to work the same works that Jesus carried out through us. Amazingly, we are to look for more! Jesus promises that we will do even *'greater things'* than the miracles that He performed so let us set our sights high (John 14:12-16)!

There are no set methods, no set formulas in Scripture and we really need to be careful that we do not fall into a methodology that hinders us from moving under the guidance of the Holy Spirit. He is the One Who will show us what action to take and when. That is why we recognise that there are means of healings not methods. We must ensure that we do not get locked into a certain way of thinking because God is not a God of methods; He is God!

Kathryn Kuhlman once shared, "just when I think that I know how God does it, He goes and does something completely different". She had recognised the infinite variety of Father's dealings with people and it is a lesson that we would do well to be mindful of.

So what means of healing can we see in the New Testament?

- Firstly, through believers in the Name of Jesus. *'These signs will follow those who believe in My Name; they will cast out demons, they will speak with new tongues, they will take up serpents and if they drink anything deadly it will by no means hurt them. They will lay their hands on the sick and they will recover'* (Mark 16:17-18).

  As believers that means demons, new tongues, snakes, poison, healing hands, that is all for us; it is part of the deal when we signed on, when God got hold of us, when we said "yes Jesus, we are going to follow You. By Your grace do something in our lives, take us on!" It is all part of the package; a very real part of the plan and we need to look to exercise all the benefits of having faith in His Name. We will examine this concept in further depth in the two later chapters addressing 'The Name of Jesus'.

- Healing can come through ministries. We are told that through the hands of the apostles many signs and wonders were done among the people (Acts 5:12) and that Stephen full of faith and power performed *'great wonders and miraculous signs'* (Acts 6:8). Whenever we meet together as a church we should have the expectancy of great wonders by the hands of the ministries and the men and women of God in our midst. When we come together on a Sunday morning, afternoon, evening or whenever it is that we meet together, let us expect something extraordinary to happen; let us expect to see healings.

Paul describes the gifts of the Spirit among which are the gifts of healings and miracles. The same Spirit distributes to each one as He wills .... *'to another has been given gifts of healing by the same Spirit and to another the effecting of miracles'* (1 Corinthians 12:7,9-10 NAS).

Of course there are a few other gifts that are mentioned there and are part of the package that we need to take hold of. The word of knowledge and the word of wisdom are often integral to moving out in healing and miracles. Remember, we are relying on the Holy Spirit's leading for each individual situation and these gifts need to come into play. Do not become boxed in and become formulaic. Let us not assume that how God worked through us yesterday will be how He intends to operate today. Let us be led by the Spirit.

- Healing comes through the elders praying the prayer of faith and anointing with oil. We are all familiar with James 5:14-15 NAS), *'is anyone among you sick? Let him call for the elders of the church, let them pray for him, anointing him with oil in the Name of the Lord and the prayer offered in faith will restore the one who is sick and the Lord will raise him up and if he has committed sins they will be forgiven him'*.

James goes on to tell us about the fellowship of believers and how healing operates in such an environment. We are to, *'confess our sins to one another, pray for one another that we may be healed. The effective prayer of a righteous man can accomplish much'* (James 5:16 NAS).

As a body together there is no need for there to be any sickness amongst us. A radical thought perhaps when I consider my reality but that is what God tells us; there should be no illness amongst us. We are to keep open accounts with each other, pray for each other and see each person healed. That needs to be our thinking, our goal. Our experience at this moment in time may say otherwise but that should spur us on to develop that healing mind-set so that it will become evident in our lives. It will become authentic as we have true, honest and vulnerable fellowship one with another. Even if I am not quite there yet I intend to be because that is the heart of Father for us.

I am challenged by a quote from Alexander Dowie, a healing evangelist from the late nineteenth century, who spoke quite bluntly; 'healing is not for Christians rather we should live in divine health'. Truly a position in God to be sought after.

- Healing comes through the eating of the bread and wine by faith, discerning the Lord's body. Paul instructs us that, *'he who eats and drinks in an unworthy manner eats and drinks judgement to himself not discerning the Lord's body. For this reason many are weak and sick among you and many sleep'* (1 Corinthians 11:27-30).

When we come to the communion table we really must not fall into the trap of treating it as just another meal, just another communion that we have taken so many times before. Even unwittingly, we must make sure our attitude is not over familiar. A few years ago a friend of ours in the church at Bordon had developed a severe gluten intolerance and even a pinch of bread would lay her low for days. She and her husband had decided that he would take the bread and wine in proxy because even that little bit of bread would cause a severe reaction. So her husband would take it in her place. I came to hear of this and the situation did not sit easy with my spirit. 1 Corinthians 10:16 tells us that we drink from a *'cup of blessing'*. We sat down together and talked it through. We came to a place of agreement that she would actually take the communion for herself and that became a significant step in the healing process. Her body did not react to the bread at all and her healing went from strength to strength.

- In the New Testament we have detailed special and extraordinary miracles. *'As a result people brought the sick out into the streets and laid them on their beds and mats so at least Peter's shadow, as he passed by, might fall on them'* (Acts 5:15).

For many years when I traveled to warmer climes I would half-jokingly declare that I enjoyed visiting such countries because it increased my opportunity to see shadow healings! England is known worldwide for our wet weather so I would tell my foreign friends, "You don't get particularly good shadows in England, so I have come here because you do! I'm expecting to see my shadow start to heal the sick because it says in the Bible that when Peter's shadow fell on the infirm as he passed by, they recovered!"

Many years went by without me being aware of my shadow falling on anyone and them subsequently experiencing healing. Yet on a cold, wet winter's day in a small gypsy church in Bulgaria where the building was illuminated by a single forty-watt bulb, something extraordinary happened. A gentleman who had responded to the call for salvation came forward. As he stood there I noticed that he had a broad smile on his face which for some reason seemed odd to me. I knew that God was doing something beyond bringing salvation to this guy and so I enquired of him, "What's going on with you?"

He explained that for some years he had been suffering from arthritis throughout his body and that the moment he stepped into my shadow he felt all the discomfort drain from his body. He lifted his arms in demonstration and said, "Look, I can bend all my fingers without any pain!" and started to open and close his hands to prove it. I realized that I might in jest have limited God to working in sunny climates with strong shadows! By His grace, I was privileged to have my heart's desire to see the Spirit work again as in New Testament times fulfilled. Even though Father had seen my longing He had wanted to show me that He was able to work way beyond my expectations and there, in a dimly lit room in a cold gypsy village in the snow, a man walked into my shadow and God healed him.

This is a lesson we would all do well to learn. We serve a God who wants us to recognize that His power is without limit and He wants to break through the paltry boundaries we place on Him working in us and through us. Let us make it our goal to no longer inhibit the Spirit's power. Let Him out of the box! During those days we held to a confession in our church which still rings true in my spirit today; "No Limits, No Boundaries", inspired by the song by Israel Houghton. Such limitations only exist in our minds.

We do not seem to hear a great deal about shadow ministry these days; you do tend to hear more about handkerchiefs and I have seen instances where tumours have shrunk under the power of God when hankies have been laid on people. Where, as we pray, the power of God is locked up in that piece of material and is then released into suffering bodies.

'God did extraordinary miracles through Paul so that even handkerchiefs and aprons that had touched him were taken to the sick and their illnesses were cured and the evil spirits left them' (Acts 19:11).

Several years ago I was preaching in Esher and a lady approached me and explained that her friend in South Africa had a massive breast tumour. The surgeons were planning to perform a mastectomy. The woman asked, "Could you pray for a handkerchief, please? We will send it in the post".

No handkerchief was to be found in the church building but they did have a clean tissue, a Kleenex. We decided that the power of God could just as easily be stored in the tissue and so we went ahead and prayed over the paper hankie. Of course, in God's economy, it is a lot cheaper to send a tissue air mail than a Marks and Spencer linen handkerchief so there is wisdom there somewhere! The tissue was duly dispatched. A few weeks later we heard from the church in Esher that the woman had received the tissue and on the morning of the operation she had been admitted to the hospital where she was scanned again to finalise the plan for the breast removal. The hospital released her because there was no longer any evidence of a tumour in her breast. After further blood tests and scans the doctors could find no cancerous cells in any part of her body! Handkerchief ministry leads to unusual and out of the ordinary miracles, bless God!

- As we have already mentioned, healing comes through speaking out the Word of God into a given circumstance which will have the effect of changing the situation. *'I tell you the truth, if anyone says to this mountain* (and let's face it sickness and disease is one big mountain in people's lives), *'Go throw yourself into the sea' and does not doubt in his heart but believes that what he says will happen, it will be done for him'* (Mark 11:23).

  'Does not doubt in his heart'. I am encouraged by this because my heart is after God and I am sure yours is too. I do not doubt in my heart that God can heal and that God will heal. My mind may be another issue which we should look to resolve but I take encouragement that Father looks on the heart.

  Paul tells us that he *'keeps asking that the God of our Lord Jesus Christ, the glorious Father, will give you the Spirit of wisdom and revelation so that you may know Him better. I pray also that the eyes of your heart may be enlightened in order that you will know the hope that you have been called to, the riches of His glorious inheritance in the saints and His incomparably great power for us who believe'* (Ephesians 1:17-18). That power is *'demonstrated in the working of His mighty strength'* (verse 19). Paul prays that the eyes of our heart will be open so that we can understand it, grasp it, be there in it, we can get hold of the *'incomparably great power and the riches of His glorious inheritance'*. Our heart attitude is to be in tune with Paul's aspirations for us.

Our inheritance is fixed and sure and the exciting thing is that we do not have to wait to enter our legacy, we do not have to wait until we get to Glory but rather it is in the here and now. We do not have to wait until they are reading the will, our bequest is to be enjoyed in the present and we are to live in the fullness of it now!

Jesus speaks to us, *'I tell you the truth, some of you standing here will not taste death before they see the Kingdom of God come with power in their lifetime'* (Mark 9:1). I want to be one of those people, how about you? I want to be one of those people who will not taste death until I have seen the Kingdom of God come with power in my lifetime. That excites me especially in the area of healing. It thrills me that we will experience the presence of the Kingdom in the here and now. We are to speak to those mountains without doubt in our heart so that we become one with the intent of the Holy Spirit that *'whatever we say'* will come to pass. Father wants a people who live in the good of this truth and so let us determine to work towards that goal.

- In the New Testament we see healings through prayer. *'Whatever things you ask for when you pray believe that you receive them and you will have them'* (Mark 11:24). *'Again I say to you that if two of you agree on earth concerning anything that you ask it will be done for you by My Father in heaven'* (Matthew 18:19).

- Which brings us to the principle known as the power of agreement. An old joke(!) but the problem is not trusting that Father will do the *'anything'* in the verse above; the problem is finding two people who will stand in agreement! However as in most jokes there is kernel of truth to be found. The power of agreement is amazingly effective and something we need to actively pursue.

    When I was working as a plumber/heating engineer I was contracted to carry out some renovation work in a home in Camberley. I was aware that the lady of the house had a son at home who was suffering with a hacking cough which was preventing him from being in school. I enquired, "What's up with the boy?" to which she replied, "He's got this terrible cough and the doctors don't know what to do about it. I can't send him to school; he's really debilitated, he's losing weight and been in and out of hospital".

Having seen various Bibles lying around the house, I pointed her to the Scripture in Matthew 18:19 and said, "I will agree with you, if you can agree with me, that by the time I finish this job your son will have recovered". The woman thought for a moment and agreed. The very next morning I was met by a much-relieved mum saying, "He isn't coughing, he's eating, he slept through the night!" The boy recovered overnight. The power of agreement is a very potent concept.

To summarise then; we have seen examples of how God heals in the Old Testament through prayer, the Word of God, signs and wonders, miracles, medical intervention and through the word of knowledge. Old Covenant practice. Specific people for specific tasks.

Now we see in the New Covenant healing through the Name of Jesus, through the ministries, through the elders, through believers, the working of miracles, the bread and wine, extraordinary miracles such as shadow and handkerchief ministry, confessing the Word, prayer and the power of agreement. God using all anointed believers for all tasks. *'By a new and living way opened for us through the curtain, that is Jesus' body'* (Hebrews 10:20).

The question is; now that we understand all these means and we see how God moves, what are we going to do? Knowledge is to be the basis from which we are to live these truths and seek to walk into a new dimension of healing power. So what do we do? That is a key question and we have already alluded to the answer. We need to be sensitive to recognising our need of being totally dependent upon the Holy Spirit and His leading. We are to discern what action we are to take in each instance to see His healing power released.

Even Jesus 'limited' Himself in the sense that He would identify a key to unlock any given situation with the help of the Spirit of God.

'Jesus gave him this answer, I tell you the truth, the Son can do nothing by Himself, He can only do what He sees the Father doing, because whatever the Father does the Son also does' (John 5:19).

'Again by Myself I can do nothing, I judge only as I hear and My judgement is just, for I seek not to please Myself but Him Who sent Me' (John 5:30).

'So Jesus said, when you lift up the Son of Man then you will know that I am He and I do nothing of My own initiative but I speak these things as the Father taught Me' (John 8:28 NAS).

We as believers recognise that we can do nothing by ourselves but that we are totally dependent on the Holy Spirit to heal and set people free. Our aim is to line up body, mind and spirit with the will of God. I want to be a person who operates in this manner, who intentionally positions myself in the way of Father's anointing and is used as a conduit for that divine unction to flow through. We do not rely on methods, we do not rely on formulas, we do not rely on what did or did not work the last time we ministered to someone. Rather we rely on the Holy Spirit's leading.

'If a man remains in Me and I in Him he will bear much fruit because apart from Me you can do nothing' (John 15:5).

So finally I would encourage you:

- Listen for His voice
- Trust your ability to hear His voice
- Do not become fearful and second guess yourself
- Do whatever He says, whatever He commands you to do
- Be expectant and look for the miracles. If you look, you will see them!

Let me tell you how our son put these principles into practice. Tom attended a course run by our church called 'The Year Team' where myself and the other ministries taught on many aspects of the Christian walk. In one particular session I had been teaching on healing and Tom returned home that evening and greeted his mother with, "Can I pray for your hearing, Mum?" to which she replied, "Yes, sure".

For the previous ten years or so Kim's hearing had been declining quite severely. She has a congenital condition which means that she has oddly shaped ear canals which have a tendency to scar over. The consultant advised her that if they operated it would likely speed up the laying down of the scar tissue. He could not estimate the extent to which her hearing would deteriorate but she had arrived at the place where she was not hearing well at all. On top of that the consultant informed us that her right ear had no intact ear drum. The scope showed just a few tattered remains.

He suggested that as she was prone to infections in that ear that it would be advisable to perform a myringoplasty. This would involve cutting out a small piece of muscle from the scalp behind the ear, scraping it down to the required thickness and then fashioning a new ear drum. A simple procedure with an overnight stay and a couple of weeks off work. The consultant said that it was unlikely to improve her hearing but it would stop infection. So he scheduled the surgery.

Tom prayed for his mother on the Wednesday evening. On the Friday, two days later, she attended the clinic for the final pre-op checks. The consultant asked, "What are doing here?" to which she replied, "Well, I received a letter. It says that I must attend for final pre-op checks" to which the doctor shrugged his shoulders and said, "But we only saw you last week!"

Kim produced the letter which emphatically stipulated 'make sure you attend both appointments'. The doctor ventured, "It must be a new system! You are having the operation in a few days' time and we don't usually see you again but as you're here, we'll have a little look".

He proceeded to pop the camera in her ear and said, "Oh". Now Kim by her own admission, being full of faith and the Holy Spirit thought, "What now? What could possibly have gone wrong?"

"Just wait there a minute" he said as he called the nurse in and asked her to go and round up his three juniors who were in clinic that day. He invited them into the consulting room and they lined up to take turns looking in her ear.

The consultant announced, "Good news, Mrs Grant, we are going to cancel the operation". Naturally, my wife asked, "Why?"

Showing her the image on the screen, he explained, "You see that bright pink area? It's a bit like if you burn yourself, the new skin underneath is red and sore? Well, we can't operate because that is a complete and intact ear drum".

Kim said, "Hang on a minute". She is seeking to be a woman of faith but can still be a bit of a sceptic! "Look in your notes. There are the diagrams, the pictures of a tattered ear drum. Yet you are saying that I actually have a perfectly complete ear drum?"

He hedged and said that he could not possibly comment on his colleagues' previous assessments etc. However as the juniors were leaving the room, one of them turned to Kim and said, "Thank you for letting me look in your ear, I have never seen anything like that before".

To which the consultant commented, "No, you really won't get to see that very often in your lifetime".

A creative miracle. My son had come home, having heard God, he trusted what God said, he did what Father directed him to do, he looked for the miracle and we saw it. Praise God!

This is the kind of people we are to be. We are to hear God and we are to trust Him. We are not to doubt and bottle it. We are to do what He says, be expectant and we will see the miracles.

Two thousand years since Abraham through to Christ. Two thousand years since Christ and the early church to now. Still today with a God that heals, still today with a God that wants to heal through us. Still today with a God that wants us to be a generation that releases healing, that sees signs following, that believes the Word of God and moves in the fullness of the truth.

We have a mandate to move ahead, building on what has gone before, learning the lessons and making the summits of the previous generations our base camp from which to launch out. Let us make sure that we are part of such a generation!

Chapter Four

The Roots of Sickness

It has been our experience that the more we have expected from Father the more expansive His works have been.

For some years, we hosted a 'Healing Hour' in our home church in Aldershot, Hampshire. We opened up the auditorium twice a week and invited people to come in. We would seek to minister to their needs either by praying with them or simply by proclaiming healing over them. These meetings were a vehicle to see Father move in healing power through us being tuned in to what the Spirit wanted to do in each one of our guest's lives. I continue to have a real sense that God wants us to lay hands on the sick in these days and heal them wherever we find ourselves.

One morning while the 'Over Fifties Coffee Club' was meeting in the foyer, one of the gentlemen came into the 'Healing Hour' after being heavily encouraged by the ladies to "give it a go"! He told us that he practised Tai Chi and mentioned that he was suffering from prostate cancer. He was on a course of monthly injections to keep the disease under control and informed us that, "they've told me that the cancer probably won't kill me. I will probably die of something else before then! The ladies have told me to come in and to get you to pray for me".

We sat down with this gentleman and ministered to him. We laid hands on him and commanded healing in Jesus' Name (Acts 3:16). When we had finished praying with him he said, "that was amazing! I felt an immense sense of peace come over me and flood through me. I'm an expert in relaxation. I've undergone medical procedures where I have just relaxed my body and felt so completely at peace and not needed any sedatives. While you were praying I felt more peaceful than I've ever felt before in my life!"

We explained, "That's great. Sometimes that sort of thing happens". We left him and he went back to the coffee morning. A week later he returned to the 'Healing Hour' to report, "It's really amazing. There was a bit of a coincidence last week".

I asked, "What do you mean by that?" to which he replied, "On the Monday after you prayed for me, I went for my monthly injection. The technician turned around to me and said, "I'm sorry sir but we can't give you the injection today".

Our friend admitted, "I have to be honest; I panicked. I thought government cutbacks, NHS cutbacks and all that! I thought that they hadn't got the drugs to give me and I said to the technician, I will die if I don't have this".

The technician reassured him and explained that "your blood test which tells us the amount of cancer in your body so we can give you the correct dosage of drug is reading in the normal range". (These readings continued to be 'normal' for the following twelve months).

The gentleman asked the consultant, "What does this mean, me coming off these drugs?" to which his consultant replied, "We don't know, I haven't taken anyone off them before but it appears that your cancer is in remission".

He said to me, "It's a bit of a coincidence that this happened after you prayed!"

Some weeks later, he came in again to the 'Healing Hour' and told us, "My legs are really hurting so I thought I would give you guys a try again! I can't walk around the town without being in a lot of pain and having to sit down and rest. I thought I'd let you do that stuff again". So the team gathered round, prayed for him and off he went only to reappear an hour later. "There's been another coincidence! I've just walked all around town, done my shopping and I'm not in pain at all". We gently informed him that this was not a 'coincidence' but rather a 'God-incidence' to demonstrate Father's love for him.

Father wants us to be a people of power and if we expect more and start stepping out and doing more for Him, He will turn up because He is committed to signs following believers.

As Jesus' disciples we are meant to be a people who are anointed with power from on high. There is a direct correlation between what our expectations of God are and what we will receive from Him and are able to accomplish for Him.

I will repeat the two questions from the previous chapters;

What are you expecting from God?
   and
What do you have?

I believe wholeheartedly that God wants us to start expecting more. To expect great things from Him and be prepared to carry out great things for Him. It is in the nature of Father to want to heal people. The Scriptures show us that He is the God Who heals us, Who takes away our sickness and restores us from illness.

Having settled these truths in our hearts, it leads us to a question;

If God's nature is so good and He is opposed to sickness then why do people get sick?

This is not a bad question to ask. Questions are not wrong. Questions are good if they are asked from the right attitude. We see this in Mary, the mother of Jesus, *"How will this be?"* she asks of the angel (Luke 1:34). Contrast this with Zachariah who asks, *"How can I be sure of this?"* (Luke 1:18). Essentially the same question as Mary's but expressed from a heart of unbelief. If we engage with Father and ask questions out of a desire to move on in God, enquiring is valuable.

I believe to ask, "why do people get sick?" is entirely valid. It is a question that often the world will ask us; "If your God loves His world why is there so much suffering and sickness?" It is a question that we need to be able to respond to correctly.

It is quite clear from Scripture that there are two forces at work in this world. Jesus tells us that, *'the thief comes only to steal, kill and destroy. I have come that they may have life and have it to the full'* (John 10:10). The thief has the sole purpose to rob people of their health and happiness. His intention is to take their joy and everything that is good and ultimately he is looking to destroy their lives. Our champion Jesus declares that He has come that we might have an abundant life overflowing in good things.

As we seek to move more under the power of the anointing of God we need to understand and be clear where sickness originates from. In doing so we are encouraged to resist disease and illness all the more fervently. Clearly here in His conversation with the Pharisees, Jesus is contrasting two works; the works of the devil and the works of God.

Let us look at Acts 10:36-38. Peter is speaking at the house of Cornelius;

'You know the message God sent to the people of Israel, telling the good news of peace through Jesus Christ who is Lord of all. You know what has happened throughout Judea, beginning in Galilee after the baptism John preached. How God anointed Jesus of Nazareth with the Holy Spirit and power and how He went around doing good and healing all who were under the power of the devil because God was with Him'.

Take note who Peter stated had power over the sick. *'They were under the power of the devil'*. Christ Himself recognised this as a fact.

The Amplified Bible states that they were *'harassed and oppressed by the power of the devil'* so clearly the Scripture teaches that sickness is a tyranny brought about by the devil. The dictionary defines 'oppression' as being 'subjugated to cruelty or force, to depress'. When you consider sickness that is exactly what it does. Disease is pitiless, it disheartens and pushes people down and robs them of a good quality of life.

The Roots of Sickness

In Luke 13:16 we find Jesus asking the leader of the synagogue, *"Should not this woman, a daughter of Abraham, who Satan has kept bound for eighteen long years, be set free on the Sabbath day from what has bound her?"* It would appear that this woman was suffering from a condition akin to osteoporosis. She was unable to stand upright and Jesus declared that she was held captive by the devil. The thief had stolen her health for nearly two decades and made her life a misery. When Jesus saw her He said, *'"Woman, you are set free from your infirmity". Then He put His hands on her and immediately she straightened up and praised God'* (Luke 13:12-13).

As we consider these passages of Scripture, we can see that Jesus leaves us in no doubt as to where He believes sickness stems from. Having accepted this truth we should seek to resist Satan's work in people's lives. On many occasions when sick people have come to me for prayer, as I have begun to resist the devil's oppression there has been a manifestation of something evil.

Jesus declared that His purpose in coming to the earth is, *'that they may have life and have it to the full'* (John 10:10). The sooner we come to the realisation that sickness and disease are not the works of God but rather are the tools of the devil then the sooner we will stop tolerating them and will start resisting them with all our might.

If someone comes into a meeting and starts manifesting we recognise it as the work of the devil and we deal with it. James

4:7 instructs us *'Submit yourselves then to God. Resist the devil and he will flee from you'*. We need to stop accepting sickness and disease and rather begin to combat the enemy behind the infirmity in every place and person where it occurs. As we do so I guarantee you that we will see people set free and healed because that is my experience.

We are to exercise wisdom when we are ministering to people. If when we are praying we recognise that the devil is involved in their lives we are to be mindful of who it is we are coming against. Obviously if you are praying with or ministering to non-Christians you need to be astute in what you say. We know who we are dealing with. We know who is the author of sickness and we know who we are coming against. Remember, he has been put under our feet! (Romans 16:20).

We need to understand the strategies of the devil. There is a battle going on and the enemy is trying to persuade us that Jesus did not really win the victory over sickness and death and that we must just expect to put up with these things as part of the human condition. Yet Isaiah 53:5 is quite clear when the prophet declares, *'by His wounds we are healed'*. Not might be healed. Not could be healed. It is; we are healed. It is already done. Do not listen to the lies of the enemy but rather resist him and see him and his works compelled to leave!

We are mindful that, *'the weapons we fight with are not weapons of the world. On the contrary, they have divine power to demolish strongholds'*. What are these strongholds? Paul continues, *'we demolish arguments and every pretension that sets itself up against the knowledge of God and we take captive every thought and make it obedient to Christ'* (2 Corinthians 10:4-5).

The devil knows that he has been beaten and disarmed (Colossians 2:15). The enemy knows that Jesus has won the battle through His death and resurrection yet Satan is still intent on preventing us from entering into the fullness of the benefits of that victory. We must be careful not to be like the two and one half tribes (Joshua 1) at the edge of the Jordan; they had come through the wilderness and could see the Promised Land yet chose to settle on the wrong side of the river. If we allow the enemy to win the battle in our minds then he will prevent us from pressing into all that we have been promised. To that end it is in our thought life that the devil will attempt to have us accept his lies and return to unrenewed forms of reasoning. It is all too easy to ignore the Word of God and to fall into unredeemed patterns of thought and for sickness to come upon us.

Several years ago a brother in the Lord did something to me that really offended. I could not fathom why he would have taken this course of action without fully intending to cause me pain. Within a few months I became completely crippled. I would sit on our sofa for ten minutes at a time trying to pick up a single sheet of paper, struggling because I could not get my fingers to work properly. I had recently returned home from Vietnam and the doctors thought that perhaps I had contracted a tropical disease whilst on my travels. Every week I was taken to the surgery for blood tests as they tried to discover, unsuccessfully, what was wrong with me. As time passed, I became more debilitated. I fell down the stairs a couple of times because joints came out of place and eventually I had to use walking sticks to get around. The problems multiplied as my arms could no longer support my weight and I was rendered immobile.

I had been prayed for numerous times but was never quite free of the problem. I attended a conference and a friend of mine came to me and asked, "Can I pray for you?" to which I replied in the affirmative.

He started to pray and then abruptly halted as he said, "God has told me that there is unforgiveness in your life."

I had to admit that this was true. I knew that I was filled with loathing for this chap who had wronged me. I explained that I could not begin to think about how to forgive him the offense and my friend asserted that it was this attitude that was causing the sickness.

I lamented, "I can't even begin to accept that there was anything good in what he has done to me". To which my friend wisely asked, "What do you value more, your health or your hatred?"

I knew that I had tried to forgive this guy but had been unable to do so. We agreed to petition Father for His help to enable me to let go of this unrighteous emotion. As we were praying, two guys came across to us and said, "Tim, Martin, can you come with us? 'X' has just fallen over and is on the floor. He has damaged his back and is in agony. We need some brothers with faith to pray for him". You can most likely guess who 'X' was! Yes, the guy I was struggling to forgive! Father was presenting me with an opportunity to let go of my unforgiveness and pray for his healing. God spoke to me; 'this is a start; forgiveness starts by praying'. I went and prayed for him and that afternoon I got complete use back in my hands. By the end of the following week the inflammation had left every joint in my body and I was returned to full health again. Praise God!

If we grant the devil room in our lives we should not be surprised if he takes advantage. People who come to us for ministry often have allowed the enemy a foothold. Sometimes unwittingly for such is the deceptive nature of the enemy. I spent time speaking with a gentleman who had come along to one of our local crusades. He was suffering from kidney failure which had damaged the nerves in his body to such an extent that he no longer had any feeling whatsoever in his legs. As I placed my hand on him to minister Father God spoke to me, "There is more to this than he is telling you".

I took my hand away and said, "Excuse me but God has told me that you're not telling me the full story".

He replied, "I knew you were going to say that!"

He went on to explain; "Ten years ago, my daughter was behaving immorally. In the end I threw her out of the house and told her to go and live somewhere else". The very next week his kidneys started to deteriorate and he was admitted to hospital with renal failure. The doctors managed to get them functioning again but meanwhile irreversible damage had affected the nerves in his legs. Time had passed and he had had no contact with his daughter for over a decade.

I related my story to him and gently encouraged him saying, "You know that you have to forgive her, don't you? This unforgiveness is at the root of the problem with your legs".

The guy left the tent that evening like a man on a mission. The next morning he returned to tell me, "I phoned my daughter last night for the first time in ten years. On recognising my voice, she asked, 'What the **** do you want?'" He explained how he wanted to apologise to which his daughter burst into tears and said, "Dad, for five years I've been trying to ring you to tell you that it's me who's sorry". They chatted further, forgiveness flowed in both directions and they agreed to meet up. He went to bed that evening and in the morning when he awoke all feeling had returned to his legs!

The enemy's mission is to steal, kill and destroy. Someone once asked Smith Wigglesworth, the great healing evangelist, why he treated people with sickness so roughly. He explained, "I don't treat people roughly. It is the devil behind the sickness that I treat roughly!" Smith understood where sickness came from.

Again, do not allow the enemy to trick you into old thinking patterns. We need to have our minds fully renewed so that we know how to conduct our lives and to recognise what the good, pleasing and perfect will of God is for us.

Paul encourages us, *'Therefore I urge you brothers in view of God's mercy to offer your bodies as living sacrifices wholly and pleasing to God. This is your spiritual act of worship. Do not conform any longer to the pattern of this world but be transformed by the renewing of your mind. Then you will be able to test and approve what God's will is. His good, pleasing and perfect will'* (Romans 12:1-2).

We are beings that are made up of body, mind and spirit. All three need to come into line with God's will for us to see His plans and purposes fulfilled.

Our mind and our body have a tendency to travel in a completely different direction to our spirit. Now and then the three line up and we see something of the fullness of God's power in that moment. Of course, Father wants all aspects of our being to be in sync at all times! We want to see more than just occasional glimpses of this in our lives.

I have always been a storyteller. One Sunday morning a sister in my congregation remarked to me, "Tim, all your stories are really old!" She was a lady that I had led to the Lord a few years earlier and my immediate reaction was, "What a cheek!"

She continued, "I've been a Christian for five years now and you're still telling the stories I heard when I first arrived. Hasn't God done anything new in your life?"

I realised that I was glorying in things that had happened in the past because nothing new was happening in the here and now. My mind was stuck on former exploits while my body had moved on in time and my spirit longed to be travelling in a different direction. Father wants us to have our body, mind and spirit all running after the same purposes because then there is a flow of power that is released through us. If we determine to bring ourselves to the place where what we do and what we think is in harmony with God's Word and what He is saying, then we will see miracles!

One summer we took twenty four discipleship students to Bulgaria and it was such a blessing to me to see miracles and significant healings almost daily at the hands of these folks as they stepped out in faith. Two of the younger team members came to me one evening and invited me to come and meet one of the children. I asked, "Why?"

They told me that this lad who was born deaf and dumb could now hear and speak after they had ministered healing to him. Totally amazing! The boy had never heard the spoken language but within an instance of his ears opening he was conversing in fluent Turkish. I could not understand a word but his mother could and that is what confirmed the healing to me. I stood and looked on at this woman weeping uncontrollably with joy at what Father God had done in her son's body.

God wants us to line up our body, mind and spirit so that His power might flow straight through us to the people around us.

If we are truly to be anointed with the Holy Spirit and power we need to be a people who are wholly submitted to God. A people who do not rely on what we see with our natural eyes or what we feel in our emotions but rather we focus on what the Holy Spirit is saying. Sometimes Father God might get you out on the edge and it may well be terrifying. That has certainly been my experience! The incidence of spitting in that lady's eyes was just the beginning of some of the seemingly crazy things that God has asked me to trust Him for. Of course, when you see people receive their healing you quickly resolve to just *'do whatever He tells you!'* (John 2:5).

There have been many times when I have felt no sense of anointing whatsoever. I could have been hitting the people over the head with a wet fish as far as my feelings were concerned! There have been other times when folk have fallen over under the power of the Holy Spirit yet when they have gotten back to their feet, nothing appears to have happened. And yet other times there has been no sense of anointing as I have laid hands on the sick and commanded them to be whole in Jesus' Name and been amazed as miracles have happened.

If you want your comfort zone tested then be in a tent filled with seven hundred people as a fist fight erupts just outside the canvas and watch in dismay as nearly all seven hundred of those people run out of the tent as you are preaching! 'Fight, fight, fight!'

Wrestle with the fact that if you are such a captivating speaker then how come hundreds have left? All that remained in the tent were my team numbering twenty-four and around a dozen or so others. This is Gypsy culture in Bulgaria! Our friend hosting the event urged, "Tim, we need to get the worship band on to draw the people back in!"

I replied, "God has just told me something".

"No, no, no! Get the band back on!" he insisted.

Under the conviction of the Holy Spirit, I maintained, "Let's just wait a second. God has shown me that there is a lady here who is blind in one eye".

I spoke out the word of knowledge to the much-reduced congregation and a woman responded. One of her eyes was completely white with no discernible iris. I placed my hand on her shoulder and started to pray.

Father spoke to me, "Tim, what are you doing?"

"Praying, Lord", I replied.

"You should place your hand over her eye and command healing", instructed Father God.

Following His instruction I covered the blind eye with my hand and declared, "In Jesus' Name, I command you to see". I took my hand away and she screamed out, "I can see!" Seven hundred people ran back into the tent to marvel at this now perfectly restored eye. We should realise that if our works are greater than the devil's works, we will get people's attention!

We cannot be swayed by what we feel or by old patterns of thinking; we have to perceive what God is saying, we need to hear His voice and act on what He commands.

Smith Wigglesworth, who I have already mentioned, is my patron saint. If you are allowed an unofficial saint, then he is mine. He was originally a plumber and as I also used to be in this line of work I feel a sense of connection with him. Wigglesworth said, "I am not moved by what I see, I am not moved by what I feel, I am only moved by what God says".

Likewise, we are not to be directed by what we see, we are not to be governed by what we think, rather we are to hear God's Word and carry out what He says. Thank God that Jesus came to destroy the works of the devil and give us life more abundantly (John 10:10). As we understand the enemy and his strategies it will help us to move and minister in the victory that Jesus has already won for us.

We need to be a people who are wholly submitted to God in every area of our being. We do not rely on what we see, we do not rely on what we feel but we rely on what the Word of God says and what the Holy Spirit is leading us to do.

While leading a mission team in Bulgaria, I came under a verbal attack from one of my travel companions who insisted that the anointing had left our current meeting because of what he considered was my 'ungodly attitude' towards him. He thought me to be out of order and an arrogant young man. I apologised by saying that if his assessment was correct, okay; but I believed that I had discerned the true reason for the Spirit's absence. Sensing a complete lack of anointing, I walked out into this meeting with the whole weight of this criticism on me.

I appealed to the folks gathered there, "We need to invite the Holy Spirit to return. We have offended Him in some way". I led the prayers to request the Holy Spirit's presence and I felt nothing tangible. I announced by faith, "We are going to now pray for anyone who is sick". Five women came forward and I was really quite fearful as I said to the first lady, "Give me your hand". As she did so it was if I had hit her over the head with a baseball bat. She was poleaxed. I moved along the line to the next lady and repeated, "Give me your hand". As her hand stretched out, I touched her and again she went down heavily under the influence of the Holy Spirit. The third woman was reluctant to give me her hand but the man standing behind her pushed it forwards and down she went. The same outcome was experienced by the fourth and the fifth women in the prayer line.

I was aware of my bodyguard stepping closer to me as a number of men were looking rather oddly at me. I asked my interpreter, "What is going on?"

He pointed to the prone women. "Look at them on the floor. The men think that you have killed them!" These guys had not seen anybody slain in the Spirit before and I have to admit that these ladies were out for the count. Several people were now coming out of the congregation and nudging the motionless women with their feet in an effort to illicit a response from them. I am worrying a little by now and am disappearing behind the bodyguard as these guys are becoming rather menacing. Thankfully, the first lady began to revive to be followed by her companions. Every one of those five women got to their feet totally healed of their ailments.

We are to be guided by God's Rhema word in every situation. It later transpired that the worship leader that evening was engaged in an illicit affair with a lady in the village. This state of affairs was offensive to the Holy Spirit and hence His withdrawal from the gathering until the situation was addressed. I was also reconciled to my brother as we sought to work through our personality conflict!

We might well look at circumstances and situations and think that we are wholly inadequate. I want to let you into a little secret; we are! It is only as we realise our shortcomings that we can rely solely on the power of God to move through us. Only then will He get all the credit because the working of miracles is not about us. It is not about having a great magazine, a snazzy website and a television programme. It is about God getting the glory. It is all about people coming to know Jesus and having their lives changed. It is about taking the ground back from the enemy who wants to steal, kill and destroy and releasing people into the fullness of life that God intended them to have.

I picture the devil as the one who is under my feet (Romans 16:20) as I have my foot on his throat. He is under our feet and yet from that position, he is screaming at us, "I'm going to beat you, just give me some foothold in your mind."

He is a liar, the father of lies' (John 8:44). Paul encourages us to *'demolish arguments and every pretension that sets itself up against the knowledge of God and we take captive every thought and make it obedient to Christ'* (2 Corinthians 10:5). The only place that the devil can have success is on the battlefield of our minds. We must allow our minds, our intellect, our reasoning to be renewed and rewired to the truth of the Word (Romans 12:2).

Several years ago we were on the streets of Kettering praying for people. I was chatting with two young lads and telling them that God heals people to which they said, "Wait here! We'll be back!"

Off they went and reappeared a few minutes later with a third boy in tow. Their friend looked a little pale and was breathless. They had obviously brought him to me in a rush.

The boys challenged me, "You say your God heals, heal him!"

I swallowed deeply. The boys went on to explain that this poor lad was not allowed to join in with any school sports activities, was not to run as he was liable to collapse because he suffered badly from asthma. "If your God heals him, then we will believe in your God", declared these young teenagers.

Having had my position of faith so roundly challenged, I began to pray for the boy and felt God direct me, "Don't pray for him."

I would encourage everyone to listen when God speaks. We might not like what He says but we should at the very least listen to His instruction!

Father reiterated, "Don't pray for him."

"What do you want me to do, Lord?" I enquired.

God explained, "I don't want you to do anything. I want him to run down the street."

Mentally, I took a sharp intake of breath. I was concerned about the boy's history of collapsing if he exerted himself. I was worried that his inhaler might not be powerful enough to ward off an attack. My mind was tied up with the natural consequences of giving the lad such an instruction. I determined to actively *'renew my mind'* and see *'what is the good, acceptable and perfect will of God'* for this boy come into being (Romans 12:2).

I spoke to the boy, "I think you should just run down the street." One of his mates asked, "Are you sure? He shouldn't do that. They've had to call the ambulance to the school when he decides to run because he has an attack."

I told the lads that I was sure that God was talking to me. The boy thought for a moment and boldly said, "I'll do it!" Off he trotted.

Father said, "He's not running, he's jogging, tell him to run."

"Give me a break, Lord, this is Kettering High Street!"

Father continued, "If he doesn't run, he won't be healed."

Ignoring the mass of pedestrians on a fine Saturday afternoon, I shouted, "I told you to run!" I tell you; I am not sure who the boy thought was chasing him but he shot off like a bullet from a gun! He ran the length of the High Street, turned and ran back to his waiting friends. There were wide grins all around as they exclaimed, "That's amazing! He shouldn't have got half-way down there without collapsing!" That evening his parents came to the meeting to find out who had made their son run down the street and cured his asthma.

Let us be mindful that prayer is not a slot machine. We put our request in the top and get the answer we are expecting out of the bottom. Prayer is to be a two-way conversation and Father desires to have that dialogue with us which is why the Holy Spirit comes into our lives. Jesus came to open the way for us to enter into the very presence of God. The veil was rent from the top to the bottom (Mark 15:38). The Almighty tore it open and allows each one of us to come into the Holy of Holies by the power of Jesus' blood (Hebrews 10:19). We must ensure that we do not put prophetic people and priests between us and God again! God wants to have a relationship with you and me. Just as on those streets in Kettering, I need to listen to His voice; I need to trust my ability to hear Him speak. Several years ago I vowed to God, "I will no longer allow fear or disappointment to stop me doing what You are saying". Some of the directives Father has given me, as you have heard, have at times sounded quite ridiculous but when I have followed His instructions the answers to prayer have been awesome. Do not allow timidity to prevent you from carrying out whatever He says and expect to see the miracle!

Remember, all sickness is from a defeated enemy. *But if I cast out the demons by the Spirit of God, then the kingdom of God has come upon you. Or how can anyone enter the strong man's house and carry off his property, unless he first ties up the strong man? And then he will plunder his house'* (Matthew 12:28-29 NASB).

Jesus went on to achieve exactly this by His death and resurrection. Our task is to plunder the enemy's 'property' by seeing sickness and disease bow the knee to Jesus and bringing release, restoration and full health!

CHAPTER FIVE

Understanding Authority

There is a Scriptural foundation of having a submissive heart attitude and surrender to Father that brings about an environment where the fullness of God's power is able to be released and effect change. Yielding our will to Father is part of the dynamic of wielding authority in any given situation that we may face.

James 4:7 tells us, *'Submit yourselves then to God. Resist the devil and he will flee from you'*. There is no doubt in my mind that the opening phrase of this verse is a key to us moving in the power of the anointing. If we are indeed to be a people who expect great things from God and are prepared to do great things for Him then we are firstly called to obedience to Father.

At every point that we find the work of the enemy in a person's life we are to believe that it is our calling to challenge that affront and see the victory that Jesus has won released into the situation.

In Matthew 8:5 we are told that, *'when Jesus had entered Capernaum a centurion came to Him, asking for help. "Lord", he said, "my servant lies at home paralysed and in terrible suffering." Jesus said to him, "I will go and heal him". The centurion replied, "Lord, I do not deserve to have You come under my roof. But just say the word and my servant will be healed. For I myself am a man under authority with soldiers under me. I tell this one 'Go' and he goes; and that one 'Come' and he comes. I say to my servant 'Do this' and he does it". When Jesus heard this, He was astonished and said to those following Him, "I tell you the truth, I have not found anyone in Israel with such great faith"'*. Then in verse 13 we read that Jesus told the centurion, *'"Go! It will be done just as you have believed it would". And his servant was healed at that very hour'*.

Notice what the centurion said to Jesus; "*I myself am a man under authority*". He did not say I am man *with* authority, but rather I am *under* authority. What the commander then went on to describe, his direction of his soldiers and slaves, would indicate that this Roman was a man who wielded influence and authority. Jesus commended this centurion's words as *'great faith'*.

The lesson here is that the centurion perceived something in Jesus that others were yet to see. People had commented that Jesus taught as someone *'having authority'* (Mark 1:22). Some had questioned by *'whose authority'* He performed miracles and forgave sin (Matthew 9:2-7) but no one had yet recognised Jesus as somebody who was moving *'under authority'* (John 12:49 AMP). The centurion goes on to explain that because he sees this in Jesus, that He was someone Who was *under* authority, he knew from his own experience that Jesus must also *have* authority. Out of this appreciation the soldier is able to make this great statement of faith when he says to Jesus, *"Just say the word and my servant will be healed"*.

I believe that the measure to which we obey authority in our lives will be the measure to which we may exercise authority. This centurion was a man of his time and perhaps he was seeking to understand Biblical concepts from a worldly perspective. When we look back at the twelve-year-old Jesus we can see that this appreciation of how the dynamic of authority works was already present in His life. In Luke 2:42-49 we have the account of the juvenile Jesus being left behind in Jerusalem. When His concerned parents found Jesus in the temple courts three days later the young Messiah simply asked, *"Why were you searching for Me? Didn't you know that I had to be in My Father's house?"* (Luke 2:49). Even at twelve years of age Jesus was not doing His own thing rather He was under His Heavenly Father's authority.

During my time pastoring the church in Bordon we would often take two cars to the meeting place to accommodate our differing schedules as parents. One Sunday lunchtime I thought that Kim had taken Tom home with her and she thought that he was travelling back with me. We were sitting in the lounge enjoying a post service cup of coffee when Kim enquired, "Where is Tom?"

"Isn't he upstairs? He didn't come home with me". At that very moment, the telephone rang and the voice on the line informed us that Tom was still at church. "Did you forget him?" Someone kindly gave our lad a lift home. As he came through the front door, he berated us, "How could you leave me behind?"

We assured him that he was in good company, "Don't worry, son; Mary and Joseph left the Son of God behind!"

In John 5:30 (NAS) we move forward in time to the adult Jesus saying, *"I can do nothing on My Own initiative, as I hear I judge and My judgement is just because I do not seek My Own will but the will of Him Who sent Me"*. The grown Christ moving under the authority of His Father.

Jesus expands further, *"I not only say the things that God tells Me to say, but I say them the way He tells Me to say them"* (John 12:50).

We would do well to not only hear Father's Word but also make sure we discern how He wishes it to be delivered. I can tell my wife, 'I love you' but it is far more meaningful if I put my arms around her as I say the words.

Jesus submitted Himself completely to His Father. Not only did He action what Father was saying He should do, not only did He say what Father was saying He should say, but He said it in the way Father God told Him to speak thus conveying all the nuance of Father's love for His people.

In the Garden of Gethsemane we have Jesus speaking to His Father, *"if You are willing, take this cup from Me. Yet not My will but Yours be done"* (Luke 22:42). The ultimate submission of His life and very earthly existence.

These Scriptures are a few examples of where Jesus constantly affirms, *"I am doing the Father's will"*. The Son was declaring that He was surrendered completely to His Father's plan.

We are to follow Jesus' example and be totally at Father's disposal regarding how we live and move. There are also other authorities that we are to recognise and allow to have sway in our lives. Jesus taught that we need to be **submitted to all authorities.** Let us take a look at the following areas;

- God's direct authority ~ *'submit to the Father of spirits and so truly live'* (Hebrews 12:9 AMP)
- delegated authority in the church ~ *'obey your spiritual leaders'* (Hebrews 13:17 AMP)
- worldly authority ~ *'be submissive to every human institution'* (1 Peter 2:13 AMP)

Some years ago, I was driving down the road and God prompted me, "You are going too fast". I reasoned, "It's only forty, Lord".

The Lord reminded me, "It's a thirty mile per hour limit". When I dawdled in easing my foot off the accelerator, Father continued, "You are still driving too fast!"

Just as I put my foot on the brake to slow down so a car shot across the carriageway in front of me, hit the car on the other side of the road which spun up in the air and landed on the truck behind me. Both vehicles rolled up onto the embankment and my car emerged unscathed. I can tell you I was saying "thank you Lord, thank you Lord" as I tended to the other drivers. It is to our advantage to obey the authorities of the land even when we feel we know better about such details as speed limits.

He has put all authorities in place and wants us to defer to them. Some Christians have a habit of saying, "I submit to God. I don't need to submit to leaders". We should not consider ourselves to be above Scriptural truths! We have to recognise that the measure to which we yield to the authorities that God has placed in our lives will be the measure to which we can exercise authority.

I attended a conference at Hothorpe Hall a number of years ago where the housekeeper came into breakfast on the last morning. She requested that we men could help the housekeeping team if we folded our bedsheets and placed them outside our bedroom door before we went into the last session. I thought, "Silly woman! Doesn't she realise that someone is going to have to unfold the bed linen to put them into the washing machine?"

So on leaving my room I simply piled the bundle of sheets on the floor outside my door and set off for the final session. The time of worship was drawing to a close and the speaker was getting up to share when Father God said to me, "You didn't fold your sheets. You're a rebel".

I defended my position, "No, I'm not, Lord! It was a senseless instruction".

Father replied, "I have put all authority in place, even housekeepers. Will you submit and fold your sheets or will you rebel?"

"Lord, I'm going back to my room!" and I set off at a run hoping that my sheets were still outside the door. I found them there and looking along the corridor I could see that there were several other piles of unfolded sheets on display. I proceeded to fold my sheets as perfectly as I could which took quite some time and then returned to the meeting. The speaker was halfway through his word and not really understanding what had just happened I settled in my seat to hear half a message!

Some months later I was praying for someone with cancer of the lung and Father God said to me, "I have given you authority to heal this person because you folded the bedsheets".

I declared confidently over the lady, "In Jesus' Name be healed!" and she was instantly cured. I shared this story on two separate occasions in two different churches. Each time a man sought me out to tell me that they had been in attendance at the same conference. Both reported, "I didn't fold my sheets either". Both of them admitted that they too had heard Father God challenge them about the bed linen and shrugged it off. They wondered with regret in their voices, "What could I have done if I had submitted?"

We do not want to miss the reward by failing to submit to God. Sometimes Father examines us to see whether we will submit to His authority and so move forward. If we fail the test, we go around the circle again and we will come back to the same place. How many tests did I fail before I grasped what God was wanting to teach me? We need to comply with the authorities in our life. I say again, the measure to which we submit to authority will be the measure to which we will move in authority.

Listen to Paul's sobering words; *'Every person should be in subjection to the governing authorities for there is no authority except from God and those which exist are established by God. Consequently, he who rebels against the authority is rebelling against what God has instituted'* (Romans 13:1-2).

Questioning the validity of the governing authority of the day is nothing new! Jesus was asked, *'is it lawful for us to pay taxes to Caesar or not? But He detected their trickery and said to them, "Show Me a denarius. Whose likeness and inscription does it have?"*

and they said, "Caesar's" and He said to them, "Render to Caesar the things which are Caesar's and to God the things that are God's" (Luke 20:22-25 NAS).

I was praying for a Christian lady in our Healing Hour and God prompted me, "She is not tithing". I said to her, "I know you have just got married and I know it's easy to forget things, but I think you have forgotten to start tithing as a married couple".

She protested, "We can't afford to do that!" I countered, "You can't afford not to". She had already informed me that she had spent £8,000 on improving their new home.

I reassured her, "I don't need your money for the blessing of the church but you need it for the blessing of your health. At the moment, your life has all the marks of not being under God's blessing".

She insisted, "We can't afford to do that". This lady then proceeded to tell me how she was avoiding paying her taxes and how she had bought replacement windows for her house and worked a deal with the fitter to avoid paying the VAT due.

"It's no wonder you're sick. You are not submitting to any authority in your life". I went on to explain that the blessings of God are conditional on us submitting to His authority. Issues such as these need to be dealt with or we run the risk of not living in the fullness of God's provision for us, including His healing power.

It is important on our journey to moving in the power of the Holy Spirit that we understand this principle and submit to all authority in our lives because in doing so we will find it releases faith and power within us.

As we have already seen, Jesus said of the centurion, *"Truly I say to you, I have not found such great faith with anyone in Israel"* (Matthew 8:10 NAS). The soldier had declared that he could see that Jesus was a man under authority and Jesus identified this as *'great faith'*. The man's recognition and understanding of authority liberated faith in him. If we want our faith to grow then we should seek to submit to authority. By recognising and understanding it, blessing and anointing are released.

Jesus taught, *'but seek first His Kingdom and His righteousness and all these things will be given to you as well'* (Matthew 6:33). The previous verses talk about clothing, food and drink. If we seek first God's Kingdom; His rule, His reign in our lives, we can trust God to supply all earthly necessities. Blessing is released into our lives alongside freedom. Peter goes further to affirm that, *'His divine power has given us everything we need for life and godliness'* (2 Peter 1:3). It is not just our physical needs that will be met but also our spiritual walk will be empowered by all that we need to move in the freedom of the Spirit.

Jesus promises us that, *"if you abide in My Word and hold fast to My teachings and live in accordance with them, you are truly My disciples and you will know the truth and the truth will set you free"* (John 8: 31-32 AMP).

Jesus' teachings put a framework in place in our lives which rather than hemming us in will see our potential fully released.

In the United States, behavioural psychologists placed a group of young children in a park which consisted of a large, grassed area with swings set in the middle. The children were allowed to play for several hours. The adults observed that the youngsters played only on the swings and did not venture far from the play equipment.

The psychologists arranged for a fence to be placed around the border of the grassed area and returned with a second group of children and repeated the exercise. They observed that the children were playing throughout the park and concluded that the newly introduced boundary inspired confidence in the children to use the whole area. The boundaries that God has placed in our lives and the aspects that He has called us to submit to Him give us the freedom to explore and enjoy the abundant life that He intends for us to have. Boundaries are not a mechanism of restriction but rather they are a security to release us to enjoy everything that He has created for us. They bring freedom.

We need to give ourselves over to the authority of the Word of God, both as it is written in Holy Scripture and as the Spirit speaks direction into our lives. We are to respect the boundaries

Father has placed in our lives knowing that they keep us safe and bring a sense of freedom. From this position we are released to exercise faith and power to affect change around us.

When I was employed as a plumber I installed a central heating system and duly presented my invoice for several thousand pounds worth of work. The householder handed me a cheque and I deposited it into my account. A fortnight later my bank manager phoned to inform me that this cheque had bounced. He had approached my client's branch manager who divulged that there were insufficient funds in the account and there was not likely to ever be enough money to cover the cheque in the foreseeable future.

That morning I had read the text in Philippians 4:19, *'my God will meet all your needs according to His glorious riches in Christ Jesus'*. I spoke to my financial consultant and he advised me to take the client to court to recover the debt. I spoke to my solicitor who told me, "You don't even have to take him to court; just take the cheque to the police station. He has committed fraud in giving you a cheque without having the funds to support it".

Yet in the back of my mind I kept on hearing, *'my God will meet all your needs according to His glorious riches in Christ Jesus'*. I chatted with my wife as I know that she is eminently sensible and always endeavours to keep me on the correct path. "Kim, I have this feeling that God is saying that He is our source of supply not this customer" which elicited the response, "that sounds right to me".

I went further, "God said to me to 'give him the job'. Don't charge him". We had spent around a thousand pounds on materials, and the remainder of the invoice was money to meet our living expenses for the month. Again, Kim replied, "sounds right to me, do it!"

We wrote to the guy and explained that we are Christians and as he clearly did not have the money to pay my bill, we wanted to bless him and to please accept your central heating system as a gift from God through us because we are confident that He will supply our needs.

Two weeks later I took a phone call from this customer. "Tim, can you come around and talk to us?" We arranged a time and I duly arrived at his home. He opened the conversation with, "I need to tell you a few things. We searched the local paper carefully for a business that was obviously a one-man band. We had several companies in to quote. You might not remember but we talked to you about your business and we discovered that you were working on your own. We did that because we never had any intention of paying your bill". He continued, "We fully understood that you are a sole trader and if we didn't pay you probably couldn't afford to take us to court. Even if you did the magistrate would only make us pay you a few pounds a month and you would probably not have the time to come and collect it or force us to pay you. We never had any intention of paying your bill".

He went on to explain, "We can't sleep at night because of your letter. We have felt so guilty because of your generosity. We have been to our building society and arranged a loan". He opened up his brief case to show me a bundle of cash; "Here is your money".

I could have had the worry of taking him to court and then the worry of him not paying the instalments. We chose to do it God's way, submitting to the authority of His Word. And Father turned the situation around!

Submitting to His authority also safeguards us against self-deception. *'Don't just listen to the Word of Truth and not respond to it for that is the essence of self-deception'* (James 1:22 TPT). We are to obey the message and to be doers of the Word not merely listeners to it. So many times I have counselled Christians who have told me that they are planning to take action which is contrary to God's Word, the Bible. As much as I have tried to dissuade them they have persisted and invariably end up in a predicament. We need to submit to the Word because it protects us from error. If we are seeking to move in power we need to have this attitude as a priority in our lives.

Submission releases God's power to us. Jesus said to the Centurion, *"Go! It will be done just as you believed it would"*. *And his servant was healed at that very hour*' (Matthew 8:13).

Understanding and obeying the authorities in our lives brings blessing. It enables God to delegate authority to us and possessing that delegated authority allows the Spirit's power to be released through us and healing to flow to set people free.

Jesus told His disciples, '*all authority has been given to Me in heaven and on earth. Go therefore and make disciples of all the nations, baptizing them in the Name of the Father and the Son and the Holy Spirit and teaching them to observe all that I commanded you and lo, I am with you always even to the end of the earth*' (Matthew 28:18 NAS).

How much authority has been given to Jesus? *All authority* has been given to Jesus and having been given that power He commissioned us and authorised us to go and make followers. Jesus tells us to teach those disciples to implement everything that He commanded us.

He charges us to go and heal the sick (Mark 16:18). He equips us with the necessary authority to carry this out. Through the past two thousand years there has always been a group of people who have gotten hold of Christ's teachings and have sought to move in signs and wonders because they have recognised that they have that assigned authority. We are a part of that group.

'Heal the sick, raise the dead, cleanse the lepers, cast out demons, freely you have received, freely give' (Matthew 10:8 NAS).

When we have been trained about authority and accepted it in our lives we shall begin to understand how we can exercise it. One day God asked of me, "If you are not moving in the full measure of authority is it because you are not submitting to authority in your life?" That is a tough question! As we seek to respond, Father releases more authority to us.

In John 14:12-13 (NAS) we read, *'Truly I say to you, he who believes in Me, the works that I do he will also do and greater works than these he will do because I go to the Father. Whatever you ask in My Name that will I do that the Father may be glorified in the Son.'* I want to reach the place where *whatever* I ask in His Name, He is going to give me. However, I know that to get to that place Father has to have the confidence that I can cope with the power that He gives me.

In times past, I have enjoyed the sport of shooting with a twelve bore shotgun. My young son would come into my study and look longingly at the weapon which was locked on the wall. "Dad", he would say, "let me fire it!" Of course, I would not consider granting such a request from a nine-year old boy. I knew that the recoil from the gun would in all probability knock him off his feet and possibly injure his shoulder. The weapon was too powerful to handle with his level of maturity. The same rationale can be applied spiritually when we are seeking to see the power of God released. We need to prove to be mature and trustworthy and skilled in handling the Word.

To reiterate; if we are to move in the delegated authority of God then we must first seek out the authorities that He has placed in our lives. Whether, in our opinion, good or bad, we are to seek to submit to them. Only then will we exercise authority in a greater measure. We would do well to take Jesus as our model and emulate His submissive attitude to the authority in His life. Paul writes, *'have this attitude in yourselves which was also in Christ Jesus Who although He existed in the form of God did not regard equality with God a thing to be grasped but emptied Himself taking the form of a bond servant and being made in the likeness of men, being found in appearance as a man He humbled Himself by becoming obedient to the point of death, even death on a cross. For this reason also God highly exalted Him and bestowed on Him a Name which is above every name so that at the Name of Jesus every knee will bow, of those who are in heaven and on the earth and under the earth and every tongue will confess that Jesus Christ is Lord to the glory of God the Father'* (Philippians 2:5-11 NAS).

We can see that Jesus did not grapple for parity with Father even though it was His right. He understood that submission to authority was not a position of inferiority and did not affect His identity. Jesus is the Son of God yet He submitted willingly to become a servant; He washed the disciples' feet that they might have an example of where to begin to serve (John 13:15) and as a result of this ethos, ultimately Jesus was highly exalted (Philippians 2:9).

When I became a Christian the one brief that the church would trust me with was to fill up the baptistry and then empty it after the service. I carried out this duty to the best of my ability and was shocked when someone else got the thanks for it! There were two of us that had been tasked but the other guy never showed up to help. One Sunday he was recognised as the church deacon because he was doing such a good job and yet he had never once put in an appearance. I moaned, "Lord, this is not fair! I am going to say something to these people about this guy! It's despicable that he should be recognised and not me!" Father replied, "I see what is done. You just submit and carry on doing what you are doing. I will raise you up in due time". Since those days I have enjoyed the privilege of traveling the world and working for the Lord in so many areas which has totally outstripped my expectations. I choose to believe that as I learnt from early on in my walk with God to be a *willing* servant so Father has entrusted me with increasing power and authority.

So in summary, to have authority we firstly need to understand it. We need to recognise that we are called to represent His authority here on earth. It is an authority that has been given to us; it has been delegated to us. We also need to find and submit to the authorities that He has placed in our lives. If we are serious about moving in power we have to be committed to obedience and have the same servant attitude that is found in Jesus. We realise that it is nothing to do with us but is everything to do with Him. We are willing servants.

It is worth repeating; I believe the measure of authority we are able to exercise is directly influenced by how well we submit to the authorities that Father has placed in our lives. Let us determine daily to actively submit to those authorities!

Chapter Six

Living by Faith

In this chapter we are going to consider the concept of faith. If we desire to be a people who seek to move more in the power of the Holy Spirit then I believe that we have to be a people who actively live by faith. In the previous chapter we examined the subject of authority and concluded that to have authority we must live our lives submitted to the agencies that Father God has placed around us.

Through the pages of this book I hope that we have come a long way in our journey towards moving in the power of the Holy Spirit and now we shall investigate the role of faith in our walk with Father God. Scripture tells us that, *'without faith it is impossible to please God'* (Hebrews 11:6) and that *'faith by itself, if it is not accompanied by action, is dead'* (James 2:17). Let us investigate this relationship between faith and works that has to be present in our lives to see the power of God released.

I believe that we have to pursue what Smith Wigglesworth termed 'ever increasing faith'. Faith is a commodity that is never static. It is either moving forward and increasing in strength in our lives or it is shrinking back. We may have been strong in faith yesterday but that doesn't automatically mean that we will be strong in faith today.

Faith is a fluid entity and must be nurtured constantly in our lives.

We need to have faith that increases. In the gospel of Matthew you will find the account of when the disciples were unable to cure a boy with a demon and Jesus had to step in and heal the lad. We read that, *'Jesus rebuked the demon and it came out of the boy who was cured at once. The disciples came to Jesus privately and said, "Why could we not drive it out?" and He said to them, "because of the littleness of your faith. For truly I say to you, if you have faith as a mustard seed, you will say to this mountain 'Move from here to there', and it will move and nothing will be impossible to you"'* (Matthew 17:18-20 NAS). Clearly the measure of our faith can hinder the power of God working through us and releasing those who are sick.

At the outset, let us look at how the Bible defines faith. Our starting point is Hebrews 11. Whenever I read this passage I am stirred up and am challenged again to achieve more for God and to see more of Him at work.

'Now faith is the assurance, the confirmation, the title deed of things we hope for, being the proof of things we do not see and the conviction of their reality. Faith perceiving as real fact what is not revealed to the senses' (Hebrews 11:1 AMP). Verse 6 continues, *'But without faith it is impossible to please and be satisfactory to Him. For whoever would come near to God must necessarily believe that God exists and that He is the Redeemer of those who earnestly and diligently seek Him out'*. Samuel Chadwick, the renowned Methodist preacher, stated that, 'Without faith, man can do nothing with God and God can do nothing with man'.

As we examine these verses we can identify several points relating to faith.

Firstly, the writer asserts, '**Now faith is....**'. The present tense. Faith is to be a current experience. As I stated above, we may have been robust in our faith in the past but it does not necessarily follow that we are strong in faith in the present. Faith needs to be a 'now' state of being. There have been times in my life where I can identify that I exercised great faith for situations. Yet there have been other times where I have faced circumstances where I have realised that I had little faith and had allowed my portion to shrink rather than having applied it and seen that measure grow. Faith 'is' and it is vital that it is a current experience.

Secondly, we can see that faith is the **substance of things hoped for**. In other words, there has to be hope present for faith to be activated. Hope is released by an intimate knowledge of God. We are all to be encouraged to deepen our relationship with Father. We facilitate that by familiarising ourselves with the Word of God that we might comprehend the very nature of God. As we better understand Father's character so hope is released in our hearts. Faith is the essence of things that are hoped for and it is the knowledge of Father's love that releases that hope and assurance to us.

Paul promises us that, *'hope does not disappoint us because God has poured out His love into our hearts by the Holy Spirit Whom He has given us'* (Romans 5:5). Hope is released to us by the work of love of the Holy Spirit and by the promises we have detailed in the Scriptures.

The apostle further prays, *'now may the God of hope fill you with all joy and peace believing that you may abound in hope by the power of the Holy Spirit'* (Romans 15:13 NAS). Father intends for us to be a people of hope. Kim will often say to me that I am one of life's eternal optimists. I would rather be an eternal optimist than an eternal pessimist! I am very much a 'glass half full' person because I am ever full of hope! I am invariably positive because when I look to God I know that He is able to do so much more than what I believe or expect of Him and that gives me great anticipation!

Let us raise our expectations of God and believe for greater works! If we shoot for the stars and hit the sky we will be doing quite well. But if we only aim for the rooftops and then hit the porch, we will be disappointed. We should live with an attitude of hope just as our Father God is the epitome of our hopefulness.

Thirdly, faith is the **evidence of things not seen**. Faith has substance, it is apparent. Faith however is not perceptible to our natural senses and moves in the unseen realm fuelled by the Word of God. There are many examples of this listed in the passage in Hebrews 11. We cannot afford to be influenced by what we see with our natural eyes. We have to put our trust in what the Word of God declares. Often you might stand believing for an outcome that you have no proof of. You may not see any evidence of a change in the situation but we are to 'see' into the unseen realm. We 'look' into what God has said and we draw that truth from the unseen realm into our physical reality. When I reached out and took hold of that pair of lungs from God's Kingdom, they were unseen in the natural. But the moment the lady with lung cancer in the previous chapter examined her most recent x-ray, the new organs became 'seen'. The gift from God had been released from the unseen realm and was now made manifest in the physical realm.

Fourthly, faith **believes that God is**. That Father is the God of every situation and circumstance and that He is both willing and has completed everything necessary for our success. God wants us to triumph! That is His plan! This truth was brought home to me while on a mission trip. In the spring we had driven down to the Balkans for two months of outreach in three nations in the Eastern Bloc. Some six months earlier, before we had set out, Father had spoken to a young lady who was at Bible School in South Africa. Father directed this girl, "When you finish here, I want you to return to England and to go on two months of mission with Tim".

She returned home from her studies and immediately signed up for the trip. She is a woman with quite a unique skill set! Lesley had previously driven tanks in Iraq for the British Army and was a fully qualified HGV mechanic. When we arrived in the Balkans both of our lorries broke down. We saw how Father God six months beforehand had prepared for our success and had spoken to this young lady to bring her all the way from South Africa to England to travel to the Balkans with us. When the vehicles broke down that did not stop us, when our generator faltered she was able to make repairs and keep our equipment fit for purpose. God had planned for our success. I want to tell you that He is planning for your success too!

Faith is an acceptance of who God is and what He is able to do. That is why it is so important that we are fully acquainted with His character and that we are aware of the depths of His very nature. Father said to Moses, *'tell them I AM sent you. I AM that I AM'* (Exodus 3:14). I *AM* whatever you need Me to be. I

AM your provider. I *AM* your healer. I *AM* the God Who can see you through. I *AM* whatever you need Me to be. I *AM* the Husband to the single parent mother. I *AM* the Father to the child without a parent. I *AM* whatever you need Me to be. Faith believes that God is!

Fifthly, faith must by its very nature **come to God**. It is clearly our responsibility to approach Father and to diligently seek after Him. James 4:8 encourages us, *'come near to God and He will come near to you'*. In the Greek this means that if we will take one step towards God, He will *run* to us. Father is looking for us to take that initial step. By its very nature, faith will propel us towards God because faith recognises that it is God that works and performs the miraculous through the power of the Holy Spirit. As we draw near we are to prove that He rewards those who persistently seek Him (Hebrews 11:6).

This is corroborated in the New Testament as we see faith at work. People came to Jesus believing that He was their healer and they determined to come close to Him often pressing through crowds. The woman with the issue of blood (Matthew 9:20) pushed through the throng to approach Jesus. She believed, *"If I can but touch the hem of His garment"* that she would be healed. Another group of guys came to the house where Jesus was teaching and because they were unable to get into the building because of the crowds, they set about ripping through the roof and lowering their paralysed friend down into Jesus' presence (Mark 2:3-12). The Bible tells us that Jesus healed *all* that came to Him (Matthew 4:24) such was His heart of compassion for the sick and needy.

So, in summary, faith is;

- a present experience
- based on hope in our heart
- has substance though it is not seen with our natural eyes

Faith is experienced out of a relationship and a knowledge of God which enables us to take hold of promises not seen and it moves those promises from the unseen realm into the here and now.

Paul declares, *'for we walk by faith not by sight'* (2 Corinthians 5:7 NAS). Sometimes the state of affairs will contradict what the Word of God proclaims and it is so important that we do not fall into the trap of allowing those circumstances to dictate our doctrine. Rather it is the Word of God that steers our beliefs and will cause our situation to come into line with that Word.

Let us now go on to consider **how faith is measurable, perceivable and most importantly is enlargeable.**

Scripture speaks to levels of faith;

- Of the centurion, Jesus said, *'he has great faith'* (Matthew 8:10)
- Of the disciples He said at times, *'they have little faith'* (Matthew 6:30)
- Of His followers He asks, *'do you still have no faith?'* (Mark 4:40)
- Of His hometown it was said that *'He could not do many miracles there because of their lack of faith'* (Mark 6:5)
- When Peter started to sink having walked on the water Jesus told the disciple that it was *'because he had little faith'* (Matthew 14:31)
- Stephen, who was stoned to death, was declared to be a man *'full of faith'* (Acts 6:5)

Would it be that we were all recognised as being men and women who are 'full of faith'!

We are to have an honest assessment of where our level of faith is which will signify our starting point.

The apostle Paul cautioned, *'for by the grace given to me I say to every one of you, do not think of yourself more highly than you ought but rather think of yourself with sober judgement in accordance with the measure of faith that God has given you'* (Romans 12:3).

God has allotted each new believer a measure of faith. The apostle encourages us to work within that measure of faith. In Ephesians 2:8, we read that, *'it is by grace that you have been saved through faith and this not from yourselves, it is a gift of God'*. The portion of faith we start out with has been given to us by Father God as we did not have anything of worth within ourselves. When we come to God at the point of salvation He graciously gives us a measure of faith. To some He apportions a large measure, to some He gives a smaller measure.

On one occasion the disciples asked Jesus, *'Lord, increase our faith (that trust and confidence that springs from our belief in God)'* (Luke 17:5 AMP). Clearly they believed that their portion of faith could be enlarged. It is possible to expand our measure as we are willing to nurture and grow our faith.

Kenneth Hagin, the great teacher on faith, was approached by a lady who declared, "the problem is, I just don't have any faith". He looked her in the eye and stated, "Well that's easy, madam. Just get saved! If you get saved, God will give you a measure of faith". Can that measure of faith be enlarged? Well as we have already seen, the disciples believed it could be as did Paul himself. He wrote to encourage the Thessalonians, *'We ought to always thank God for you brothers and rightly so because your faith is growing more and more and the love every one of you has for each other is increasing'* (2 Thessalonians 1:3).

So we have the disciples asking Jesus to increase their faith and here we have Paul recognising that the faith of the church at Thessalonica is growing. It is so important that our faith continues to grow. The question is, how does that happen? How do we increase our faith?

Let us revisit Luke 17: 6-8 (NAS) and see how Jesus answered the disciples; *'If you have faith as a mustard seed you can say to this mulberry tree, "be uprooted and planted in the sea" and it will obey you. Suppose one of you had a servant ploughing or looking after the sheep. Would he say to that servant when he comes in from the field, "Come along now; sit down to eat?" Would he not rather say, "Prepare my supper, get yourself ready, wait on me while I eat and drink and after that, you may eat and drink"?'*

My experience tells me that many people fail to understand what Jesus is teaching in this passage. The verses are used to justify the limitations of their faith.

Jesus had replied, *'if you have faith as a mustard seed …..'*. The disciples had asked Jesus to increase their faith as they recognised that it is not appropriate to settle for the minimum you might get away with!

Jesus teaches that it does not matter what you start with. It can grow to a place where whatever you say will happen, even down to telling a tree to throw itself into the sea. Yes, a mustard seed is small yet within that seed is the potential for it to grow into something which is much, much bigger. He spoke of a mustard seed being akin to the Kingdom of God planted in the ground such that it grows into a tree so large that the birds of the air may come and nest in it (Mark 4:30-32).

Mustard seeds have the potential for boundless growth locked within them. The spiritual reality is that if we have *'faith as a mustard seed*' we can see increase released and great things accomplished. It doesn't matter what we start with, it matters where we finish!

So, what must we do to see our faith grow? I liken my faith to a muscle. If you want to build up your muscles then you have to work them. Likewise, we have to actively work our faith and look for opportunities to do so. Faith is a spiritual muscle that needs a constant work out.

As part of a weight loss programme I joined a gym with another local minister who had also decided to try to increase his level of fitness. We attended a training evening to learn how to operate all the pieces of equipment and returned a couple of days later for our first session. We changed our clothes and stepped into the gym and were just debating which piece of equipment to tackle first when the door behind us opened.

A guy with the physique of Mr. Universe strutted into the room. He was wearing a shirt which was cropped at the arms to show off his impressive biceps and the rest of his body was similarly toned. He had muscles where I did not realise anyone could have muscles and as he walked into the gym he looked us up and down. It was quite clear from his expression that he was metaphorically kicking sand in our faces as we stood on our beach! It was rather obvious that we were new to the gym and he was going to show us what he was all about. He put his hand in his pocket and pulled out a metal pin. He strode over to a machine where you sit on a bench and use your arms to lift a stack of weights positioned behind you. He made a great show of putting his pin in the very bottom setting which meant he would be lifting the maximum weight. He sat down, raised his arms to the pads and in quick succession lifted the weights three times. Sweat poured off his body as he stood up, sneered at us and walked back out the door. I looked at my friend and foolishly remarked, "he only did it three times!"

I found my pin and popped it in the bottom weight. I sat down and thought, "I can do this!" I readied myself as I put my arms up and tried to lift the weights. After several fruitless seconds, my friend called out, "Stop! You're going to burst a blood vessel!" The weights had not moved a single millimetre.

I quickly realised that I needed to start where I was. The apostle Paul advises us to have a *'sober opinion of yourself'* (Romans 12:3 NAS). We are to work within the measure of faith that we have. I learnt that day that I was not in any kind of shape to lift all the weights. As I regularly exercised my muscles grew in size and I began to lift successively more of the load.

In this story of a servant working in the field Jesus pointed out, 'when your servant comes in at the end of a day, you don't say to him "sit down and have a meal". No, you say to him, "get yourself washed up, get yourself cleaned up, get in the kitchen, cook my dinner, then come and serve me". When that servant has done everything you require of him, then he can have a rest'.

It is imperative that we seek to work our faith every day. The more we exercise it, the more our measure of faith will grow.

All too often the devil will challenge us; "see that person with cancer/multiple sclerosis/arthritis? You call yourself a believer; go and heal them". The trouble is, every time we have a headache, we reach for the paracetamol. We rather should see that minor ailment as an opportunity to exercise our faith in order to grow it. So that when we are confronted with a more serious scenario we are able to respond with confidence because we have already proven our faith muscle to be effective. The 'father of lies' loves to entice us into situations beyond our measure of faith and often we simply end up damaging ourselves when nothing perceivable happens. Rather we should move in accordance with the measure of our faith.

Be encouraged, we are not to shrink back, we do not settle for an inadequate measure! We may start at square one and say, "God, I am going to pray for the situations that I have faith for. I will bless the people that I don't have faith for yet and I will stand with them to the measure of my faith. Help me increase my faith". As I have taken this position and sought to push the boundaries so my faith has grown. I am not satisfied with where I am now. I am still pushing and I am not letting my faith rest.

At times, Father will say to me, "you need to move in faith again, son". One such instance was when we were praying about Kim giving up work so she could be more involved with my ministry. She was earning a reasonable salary which helped cover our bills and naturally speaking we would not be able to manage without it. We were praying that God would supply the finance so that she could resign her job but we were yet to see Father's provision come through. We were eating breakfast with a Christian minister, Ian, who was staying with us for the weekend when he said to me, "Tim, God's told me that He will meet all your needs".

I asked, "Why do you say that?" to which Ian replied, "I just have a feeling that you have a project on the go at the moment where you have a need".

"I do. I want Kim to give up her job so that she can work and travel with me but we need her salary".

"It's not a need. She's working, so you have no shortfall at the moment. When it becomes a need then He will supply it", Ian wisely directed.

We discussed this faith challenge and agreed that the next day Kim would go into school and hand in her notice. We now had a need! We now had an opportunity to see our faith grow!

At that time we had been trying to sell my parents' retirement apartment for over a year since their death and there had been no market interest. That week, Kim's mother phoned to ask if she could buy the flat if it was still available! The deal was struck which enabled us to clear our mortgage which accounted for half of Kim's salary. Shortly afterwards, I was in our regular leaders' meeting when Derek approached me and said, "Tim, I really feel that we should support Kim to some extent. I am going to suggest to the trustees that we start giving you an extra £5,000 per year". This meant that the best part of 90% of her salary was now covered. To add to our blessing, Kenneth Copeland Ministries sent us an unsolicited gift of £1,000 which covered Kim's flight expenses for the coming twelve months. Father had provided for our needs as we moved out in faith. Bless His Name!

We have to work our faith which is often challenging. Occasionally, I will ask God to give me a break, let me have a breather and let me rest my faith. Father says, "the trouble is, son, when you rest your faith, not only does it stop growing, it shrinks back if you don't use it. You don't stand still, you go backwards". Living by faith is not always a comfortable place to be but then Jesus never promised that it would be! If we want to see miracles then we need to get used to it! God is going to be pushing our boundaries every day and the more we respond the more we will see.

We have likened our faith to a muscle. To build up a muscle you do two things; you exercise your body and you feed your body with the correct fuel. Over the years we have had the privilege of working with a company of London hard men called 'Tough Talk'. They are a group of EastEnders who share the message of Jesus. Whenever they visited I would love spending time with them because I could sit there looking small against their bulk.

They are big guys, all muscle. They feed their bodies well and exercise them vigorously. They are impressively muscular and carry out feats of power lifting. These men are awesome and trophies of God's grace.

I decided that I was going to bless them because they had worked with me on several occasions and though we had always given them a gift this time I wanted to bless them further. I offered, "Let me take you out for dinner".

That evening we arrived at a local restaurant and as our waitress distributed the menus I said, "Guys, just have whatever you want". Big mistake! The leader of the group picked up the menu and he called the waitress over and he began to order dishes. I thought, "that's strange, he's ordering for everyone". He certainly had an eye for the best on the menu. "I'll have the 8oz sirloin steak, I'll have the 12oz rump steak, I'll have this and I'll have that". He then passed the menu to the next guy who began to order his meal! Meanwhile I am wondering, "have I enough money in my wallet? Have I got my credit card with me?" As these guys ate their way through a mountain of food I began to understand that you can work your muscles but unless you feed your body with the correct nutrition you are not going to grow those muscles. These men fed their bodies well and then exercised to turn those calories into useful muscle.

Spiritually, if we are to build our faith we not only need to exercise that faith but we need to ensure that we feed our faith with the right food. We find the second key to seeing our faith grow where Paul says, *'Consequently, faith comes from hearing the message and the message is heard through* **the Word of Christ**' (Romans 10:17). Just as a body builder needs to exercise his muscles to see them grow, so he also has to eat the appropriate kind of food to fuel that increase. Just as we need to work our faith, so we also need to feed our faith. We need to feed our faith on the Word of God. As we nourish our spirit and exercise our measure of faith so that measure of faith will grow.

However we must recognise that there are **enemies to our faith**. Stumbling blocks that are in place to seek to prevent us from becoming all that Father God intends us to be. Let us consider the parable of the sower. Jesus explains that *'the worries of this world and the deceitfulness of riches and the desire for other things enter in and choke the Word and the Word becomes unfruitful'* (Mark 4:19 NAS). If the purpose of the Word is to feed our faith but it has become unfruitful, what has happened? What has caused our faith to fail to thrive? We see three enemies to our faith here in this account;

- The *worries of this world*. Too often we can fall into the trap of being anxious about worldly concerns. In a climate of economic recession we can get caught up with being worried about our daily needs and it has the potential of distracting us from the Word. That very Word where Jesus assures us regarding food and drink, clothes to wear and our most basic necessities; *'your heavenly Father knows that you need all these things'* (Matthew 6:25-32 NAS).

- The *deceitfulness of riches*. In these times I think that the world is discovering that security does not come from relying on your bank balance. Some time ago I read an article about a former Chief of Police of the Northern Ireland Constabulary who had transferred his life savings from his pension fund into his bank account. The bank failed and the chap discovered that they were not covered by the Government scheme that bailed out most banks at that time. Everything that he had put his trust in for his retirement was gone in a moment. There is a deceitfulness to riches. Wealth promises much but often may fail to live up to its potential and bring little lasting satisfaction to our lives and the lives of others.

When I was a pastor in Bordon I shared an office building with a number of social agencies and together we employed a cleaning lady for the complex. I have to say that she exhibited somewhat less than a sunny disposition. She was a worrier and was always concerned about how much money she and her husband were spending, how much debt they were in and above all these issues, she was frightened that her husband was going to leave her. One Monday morning she failed to turn up for work and we all wondered where she was. We were concerned that she might be ill. She neglected to arrive the next day and by the Wednesday we were aware of a rumour that was circulating locally. Evidently on the Saturday evening her numbers 'came up'. This lady won 2.5 million pounds courtesy of the National Lottery! No wonder she missed work! I never saw her again but I did hear her being questioned on the radio sometime later. The interviewer asked, "Has winning the lottery changed your life much?" I found her reply to be one of the saddest things; "Winning the lottery hasn't changed my life much at all. I used to worry about how much money we were spending. I still do, we are just spending more. I used to worry about our debts. Our debts are just bigger now. I used to worry that my husband would leave me. Now I am certain that he will because of all these young girls who are chasing after him and flattering him when they are just after his money". She concluded, "Winning the lottery seems to have just made things worse for us".

Yet every Saturday evening millions of people wait for those balls to drop out of the machine that they might have their lives changed. There is a deceitfulness to riches that will try to steer our focus away from God's Word and if we allow that to happen then the Word becomes unfruitful in our lives. Father is happy for us to enjoy fine possessions but the onus is on us to ensure that those material riches do not distract us. We are to be focussed on seeking first His Kingdom and His Righteousness and Jesus promises that *'all these things shall be added to you'* (Matthew 6:33 NAS). Riches are attractive but unless we have the Holy Spirit settled within us to bring true joy and happiness then fleeting pleasures and treasure will not affect a permanent change to our lives.

- The *desire for other things*. We can become fixated on what we yearn for; a lovely home, an expensive car, building a career or indeed whatever floats your boat! Father is happy for us to realise those aspirations but we must always find our prime motivation from following His plans and purposes for our lives.

Let us further consider the account of when Peter sees Jesus walking on the Sea of Galilee. The disciple calls out, *"'if it's You*

Lord, call me to come and I will come". And He said, "Come"'. Peter climbed out of the boat and walked on the water and came towards Jesus. I want you to appreciate that Peter *walked* on the water: this fisherman was performing the impossible! The account continues, *'Then he saw the wind and was afraid and beginning to sink he cried out "Lord save me!" Immediately Jesus reached out His hand and caught him. "You of little faith", He said, "Why did you doubt?"'* (Matthew 14:29-31). Here are a further two enemies of our faith;

- *Circumstances* and *worldly wisdom*. Here we have Peter and he is walking on the water. Can you imagine it? There he is, splash, splash, splash, and then he takes his eyes off of Jesus as he became aware of the strong wind. Now as we know, Peter was a fisherman. He had acquired worldly wisdom, plenty of experience of such conditions and here he looks at the wind and I imagine that he reasoned, "hold on, if I was out in a boat today and I saw that wind I would be thinking that I should be getting back to the shore in a hurry!" *'He saw the wind and he became afraid'* (verse 30). His natural wisdom clicked in and fear displaced faith.

    Often we can step out in faith and be seeing the miraculous and the enemy will seek to interfere. We take our eyes off of Jesus and in that moment we start to sink because our natural wisdom kicks in. Worldly wisdom.

Peter became afraid. Fear and faith are opposites. The enemy wants to sow uncertainty, hesitation and scepticism into our lives. The father of lies will challenge you, "You shouldn't be doing this. What will happen if nothing changes?" When we are seeing the supernatural unfolding before us we should not get side-tracked by natural patterns of reasoning that the enemy will try to exploit.

Smith Wigglesworth stood in front of a woman in a wheelchair and the preacher heard the voice of the Spirit whispering to him, "Smith, grab this woman and command her to walk in Jesus' Name". Wigglesworth later described how immediately another voice spoke in his ear saying, "What happens when she doesn't walk?" Wigglesworth grabbed the woman by her gown, dragged her from the seat, stood her up on her feet and commanded, "Walk!" and she began to walk. Smith addressed the second voice, "Satan, what happens to you now? She's walking!" The enemy will try to sow fear of failure, ridicule or embarrassment to diminish our faith.

I brought this teaching to a group of teenage boys and girls in Bulgaria. These youths were no older than fifteen years of age. We had invited the pastors to come to hear these principles and they failed to show up. However, there were a whole gaggle of youngsters hanging around and I asked them, "Do you want to hear the teaching?" They sat down and we shared with them.

In the tent that evening I announced to the congregation, "We are not going to pray; the English people are not going to pray for the sick tonight. We have taught these young men and women to pray for the sick. They are going to come and pray for you". I have to say that we were surrounded by some very disgruntled faces. "We don't want them praying for us", they grumbled. They had little respect for these youngsters. The crowd were looking with their natural sight rather than with eyes of faith.

There was a great push in towards the English team to try to convince us to lay hands on them rather than receive from the teenagers. Looking around I was unable to spot the youngsters anywhere. Earlier in the afternoon when we were opening the meeting we saw some of these young people carrying a boy into the tent who obviously was unable to walk. We could see that his legs looked as if they were boneless and made out of rubber. The limbs bent in ways they really should not. They brought him under the canvas while pushing his wheelchair over the uneven ground. They gently sat him back in his chair to one side of the tent.

Unbeknown to me, when the crowd had pushed forward to persuade the mission team to pray for them, the young gypsy boys and girls had run to their friend. I become aware of a Mexican wave of applause starting from the other side of the tent. I am surrounded by people; I do not understand what is going on and I am desperately trying to see what all the fuss is about. A gap clears and I spy this young lad walking around the tent, not particularly gracefully, but he is walking and I realise in a flash that this is the boy that had been carried in. He is now standing on these legs that previously could not hold his weight. Not only is he standing on them, he's walking on them! I rush over and ask the youngsters, "What did you do?" They replied, "We only did what you taught us". I exclaimed, "I didn't teach you that!" "Oh yes you did!", they replied. "You told us about that man named Smith who just grabbed the lady from the wheelchair, stood her on her legs and said 'walk'. So we came over to our friend, grabbed him by his shirt, dragged him from his chair, stood him up and said "Walk!" and now he's walking!" They had no fear. They exercised faith. They were not distracted by their elders' attitude towards them. They focused on Jesus and saw their miracle. "Man", I thought, "I need to learn my own lessons!"

- *Doubt.* Jesus asked Peter, *'Why did you doubt?'* The enemy loves to try and sow unbelief in us when we declare healing; will it happen, won't it happen? We need a measure of that Wigglesworth spirit; it will! We need an ever deepening relationship with Father God and it is only out of this relationship that doubt is diminished.

We will overcome all the enemies of our faith in one unfailing way. The writer to the Hebrews instructs us, *'fix your eyes on Jesus, the author and perfecter of your faith Who for the joy set before Him endured the cross, scorning its shame and sat down at the right hand of the throne of God'* (Hebrews 12:2).

All five of these adversaries are overcome in this simple act; that we focus our eyes back on Jesus. When you feel fear rising in you, look back to Jesus. When you start to doubt, look back to Jesus. When concerns of this life crowd in, look to Jesus. He is the source and is the One Who gave us our faith and He is the One Who will perfect our faith. It was only as Peter took his eyes off of Jesus and began to look at the conditions around him that he started to sink. When you are already achieving the impossible, surely what is happening around you is inconsequential! Faith is a road we tread every day. We have to step out in faith, we must exercise our faith and we are required to feed our faith. The result is a growing and dynamic measure of faith.

Paul writes, *'Brethren, I do not regard myself as having laid hold of it. Yet one thing I do, forgetting what lies behind and reaching forward to what lies ahead, I press on toward the goal for the prize of the upward call of God in Christ Jesus'* (Philippians 3:13-14 NAS). I want to encourage you to have the same attitude. Let us work our faith. Let us overcome the enemies by keeping our eyes fixed on Jesus and let us see our faith increase.

As our faith grows and we are submitted to the authorities that God has placed into our lives then nothing will be impossible to us. We must ensure that we have a sober judgement of where we are in our walk of faith and then seek to move on from there.

Never fail to realise the potential of the measure that God has already invested in you! We are to recognise that Jesus is the One that gave us our faith and that He is the One Who will complete our faith. We are to take on board the simple principles that He has given us and as we apply our measure of faith and keep on using it, so it will grow stronger. As we feed on the Word, faith will grow stronger yet. Ultimately we will become the men and women who are a people of power and we will see the miracles and marvellous exploits that the Word promises us.

The more I have expected from God, the more I have seen from God. The more I have worked my faith, the more my measure has grown. The more I have fed my faith correctly, the more hope has increased within me. Nothing is impossible! Under the New Covenant we have become a royal priesthood (1 Peter 2:9) where all of us as sons and daughters of the most High God (James 1:18) can move in power. We simply need to commit to learning the lessons. Growing in faith is simple though it may not necessarily be easy. There is often a price to be paid. Sometimes He might just ask you to 'fold some sheets'! I would encourage you not to miss the opportunity because as you submit to Him you will release His authority and who knows what Father God will empower you to accomplish?

Chapter Seven

The Name of Jesus part 1

The Name of Jesus is a powerful concept which warrants examination. Throughout the New Testament we come across the words, *'In My Name'*, *'In Jesus' Name'* and *'In His Name'* in a variety of situations. We have Jesus Himself instructing us, *'Whatever you ask in My Name that will I do, that the Father may be glorified in the Son. If you ask Me anything in My Name, I will do it'* (John 14:13-14 NAS) and again, *'Truly, truly I say to you, if you ask the Father for anything, He will give it to you in My Name'* (John 16:23 NAS).

In Scripture we see that speaking the 'Name of Jesus' was used in a variety of contexts.

- **Salvation** comes in His Name, *'for there is no other name by which we must be saved. There is salvation in no one else'* (Acts 4:12 NAS). This is such an unambiguous statement that rather flies in the face of the universalistic thinking we hear so much of in the world today. Thinking in general society is that all roads lead to God. Scripture is unequivocally clear that all roads do not! Paul reminds us of the words of the prophet Joel that only those that, *'call on the Name of the Lord will be saved'* (Romans 10:13). There is no other legitimate avenue to experience new life.

- We are to **baptize disciples** in His Name. The Great Commission, *'Go and make disciples of the nations, baptizing them in the Name of the Father and the Name of the Son and the Holy Spirit'* (Matthew 28:19 NAS) is clear. The imperative to go and make disciples is followed immediately by the instruction to baptize them so that they might be identified by the world as followers of Jesus. This public act of confession of faith in Jesus as their Lord and Saviour was a transparent declaration of their future walk and embracing of their changed status.

- We are **justified, washed and sanctified** *'in the Name of the Lord Jesus Christ'* (1 Corinthians 6:11 NAS). We have been saved from this world and are being made fit for His Presence by the work of the Holy Spirit in our lives.

- In the **subjugation of demons**. The seventy disciples sent out by Jesus had returned and reported back to Him. They were ecstatic with joy that *'even the demons obeyed us when we commanded them in Your Name'* (Luke 10:17 TPT). After His resurrection Jesus commissioned His followers to drive out demons. *'These signs will accompany* *those who have believed; in My Name they will cast out demons'* (Mark 16:17-18). That was the disciples' mandate and their mission. Today it is still the assignment of believers everywhere to see the people of this world set free from the effects of the works of the enemy.

- Paul instructs us that the revelation of God in the words and **life of Jesus** is to be the guiding set of principles by which all believers should live, *'Whatever you do in word or deed, do all in the Name of the Lord Jesus'* (Colossians 3:17 NAS).

- And finally, for the subject of this book, we see that **healing** occurs in His Name. As exampled by Peter at the Beautiful Gate, *'silver and gold I do not have but that which I do possess I give to you; in the Name of Jesus, walk!'* (Acts 3:6 AMP) and where before the elders and priests Peter declared, *'let it be known to all of you and to all the people of Israel that by the Name of Jesus Christ the Nazarene Whom you crucified, Whom God raised from the dead – in this Name this man stands before you in good health'* (Acts 4:10 AMP).

So, we see that Jesus has invited, urged and has commanded us to ask in His Name and has promised incredible results! Those verses in John 14 and 16, *'whatever you ask in My Name .... Ask anything in My Name and He will give it to you'*, are some of the most powerful verses in all of Scripture. But what does it mean to minister in the Name of Jesus? When we ask for, pray for, declare healing in Jesus' Name?

Firstly, we are acknowledging the shortcomings of our own name, position or influence.

When I minister in Jesus' Name I come boldly before God because of the power of *His* Name. Our daughter was married a few years ago and putting all modern fads aside, she has taken her new husband's name. Grant has changed to Pritchard. Two have become one and all their worldly possessions are now shared and Becky is able to have every advantage that becoming a 'Pritchard' entails. Quite what that means, only time will tell!

We, the church, are the Bride of Christ and we are now joined with the Bridegroom. We have made ourselves ready by clothing ourselves *'in fine linen, bright and clean, for the fine linen is the righteous acts of the saints'* (Revelation 19:7-8 NAS). We have had a name change and now are party to all the benefits and advantages that come with that change of identity. We no longer act in our own name but rather in His, Jesus the Bridegroom. And in comparison what we brought to the table is worthless compared to the glory and power of our Lord Christ Jesus.

Secondly, we identify with the person of Jesus Christ.

Jesus has literally given us His Name. When I use that Name, I am confessing that He is mine and that I am His. I am a *'fellow heir with Christ*' (Romans 8:17 NAS). It is akin to visiting the bank of the Kingdom knowing I have nothing deposited there. If I go in my name I will receive absolutely nothing. But Jesus Christ has unlimited funds in the bank of the Kingdom and He has granted me the privilege of going to that bank with His Name on my cheques. Everything is released to me. Whatever I need in any area of my life is readily available to me to freely access.

We can draw from a different Kingdom, a Kingdom that He has made us a part of. Paul tells us that we have been '*created for good works which God has prepared beforehand that we should walk in them*' (Ephesians 2:10 NAS). Just as in my story of folding the sheets when Father told me that 'because you have submitted yourself to the housekeeper's authority, I have allowed you to take that new pair of lungs from My Kingdom and give them to this lady with lung cancer'. One of the good works that God had prepared for me to act on. What miracles of healing has Father got lined up for you? Which acts of healing have been earmarked for you? We have a new identity as the Bride of the Lamb and we can legitimately act in the power of His Name.

As Jesus has told us, '*it is not you who speaks but it is the Spirit of the Father Who speaks in you*' (Matthew 10:20 NAS). We identify with the person of the Godhead Whose family Name we carry.

Thirdly, we minister in His authority.

There is an anecdote set in America of a traffic cop who sat down at the side of the road for a rest. The day was hot and he removed his cap to mop his head. The story goes that along came a child who picked up the policeman's hat, wandered out into the busy junction and began to direct the traffic. Amazingly, the people in the cars followed that youngster's direction because they respected the office, the position of authority designated by that cap. They did not see a young boy rather they responded to the badge on that headgear. A charming tale or possible urban myth?

To minister in Jesus' Name is to ask by His authority; and to ask by His authority is to ask in accordance with His will as revealed in the Word and by the Holy Spirit. Just as with the disciples where we read that Jesus *'gave them power and authority over all the demons and to heal diseases'* (Luke 9:1 NAS), so we are able to minister in His authority. Nothing of us rather all of Him as His authority has been delegated to us. Why?

Because, fourthly, we submit to His will.

Jesus' authority rested with His submission to the Father and so likewise, our authority rests with our submission to Him. To ask in Jesus' Name is to ask according to His nature and His nature is one of submission. We are all familiar with Philippians 2:6 which says, *'although He existed in the form of God, Jesus did not regard equality with God a thing to be grasped but rather took the form of a servant and humbled Himself*. His was a nature of submission to Father's will. If you refer to the opening pages of this book, you will find the nature and character of God discussed there. How we are to recognize and assimilate all that God is into our own lives and character. Jesus submitted to His Father's will as should we. Paul reminds us that, *'we live by the Spirit so let us walk by the Spirit. Let us go forward walking in line, our conduct controlled by the Spirit'* (Galatians 5:25 AMP). We are to live lives that are influenced and directed by the Holy Spirit.

Fifthly, we are representing Jesus and His interests here on earth.

The world is unable to see Jesus but they should be able to see Jesus in us His followers.

It is much the same as the legal arrangement known as the power of attorney. My mother-in-law was well into her eighties and was getting rather forgetful. There ensued a discussion between my wife and her brother and sisters about having 'power of attorney' to safeguard their mother's wellbeing and affairs. In such matters one person may represent the interests of another in their absence. They have been given the legal right to act lawfully on their behalf and in accordance with their wishes.

Jesus has given every believer unlimited and general power of attorney in all matters of the Kingdom and the right to use His Name in every situation.

Sixthly, we are to be expectant.

When we minister in Jesus' Name we are to expect the answer in accord with the value of His Name. Paul stipulates that the Name of Jesus *'is above all other names'* (Philippians 2:9).

I love the passage in the New Testament where the apostle Paul tells us that Jesus is *'far above all rule and authority and power and dominion and every name that is named not only in this age but also in the one to come. And God has put all things in subjection under His feet and gave Him as head over all things to the church which is His body, the fullness of Him Who fills all in all'* (Ephesians 1:21-23NAS).

Everything comes under the rule of authority and the power of Jesus. We as the church, His body here on earth, are to act with that same measure of authority because Jesus has filled us up with Himself. *'We have the mind of Christ and hold the thoughts, feelings and purposes of His heart'* (1 Corinthians 2:16 AMP) so that we might successfully implement His intentions here in the world.

We are to know what He is thinking, how He feels about situations and act upon the purposes of His heart. We can act with the power and authority which He has filled us up with as we submit our lives to Him and give ourselves over fully to His will for our lives.

This is such an exciting prospect! Imagine, dare to start to imagine, just what we could accomplish in His Name.

What chains of disease we could see broken, what fetters of infirmity we could see shattered, what sickness we could see healed because we choose to take Him at His Word!! Because we appreciate and acknowledge that as His disciples we are *'filled up to the very fullness of God'* (Ephesians 3:19 NAS).

We are equipped and have been given the right to act in the glorious Name of Jesus. We can pray and minister with great and excited expectation!

CHAPTER EIGHT

The Name of Jesus part 2

Let us return to Acts 3 and take a further look at the first miracle that we have recorded after the disciples were filled with the Holy Spirit. This account has much to tell us about understanding the anointing of the Spirit and being the people of power that we are called to be.

'Now Peter and John were going up to the temple at the ninth hour, the hour of prayer, and a certain man who had been lame from his mother's womb was being carried along whom they used to set down every day at the gate of the temple which is called Beautiful, in order to beg alms from those who were entering the temple. When he saw Peter and John about to go into the temple he began asking to receive alms but Peter, along with John, fixed his gaze on him and said, "look at us" and he began to give them his attention expecting to receive something from them. But Peter said, "I do not possess silver and gold but what I do have I give to you; in the Name of Jesus Christ the Nazarene walk". And seizing him by the right hand he raised him

*up and immediately his feet and ankles were strengthened. With a leap he stood upright and began to walk and entered the temple with them walking and leaping and praising God. And all the people saw him walking and praising God and they were taking note of him as being the one who used to sit at the Beautiful Gate of the temple to beg alms and they were filled with wonder and amazement at what had happened to him. While he was clinging to Peter and John all the people ran together to them at the so called portico of Solomon, full of amazement but when Peter saw this he replied to them "men of Israel, why are you amazed at this or why do you gaze at us as if by our own power or piety we had made him walk? The God of Abraham, Isaac and Jacob, the God of our fathers has glorified His servant Jesus, the One Who you delivered and disowned in the presence of Pilate when he had decided to release Him but you disowned the Holy and Righteous One and asked for a murderer to be granted to you but put to death the Prince of Life, the One Whom God raised from the dead, a fact to which we are all witnesses. And on the basis of faith in His Name it is the **Name of Jesus** which has strengthened this man whom you see and know and the faith which comes through Him has given him this perfect health in the presence of you all'* (Acts 3:1-16 NAS).

A recurring theme throughout this book includes our response to the question; 'What are you expecting from God?' In our discussion of the topic we have explored what we have to give to those who are under attack by the devil as he seeks to inflict sickness and disease upon them. We continue to seek a greater understanding of what we have in God that we might see those who have been oppressed set free and given true liberty. This is Father's intention for people everywhere. He desires for us to partner with Him in bringing that release. He expects us to be a people of power. We need to encourage each other to step out even more boldly than we have dared to before. Our attitude is to be one of expectation of greater feats from Father and to be prepared to carry out even more marvellous deeds for our God.

We would do well to make such a confession over one another and to stir each another up to accomplish the miraculous for Father God. As we confess with our mouths, faith stirs in our hearts and we start to flow in the good of what we have declared. Jesus promises us that we will have whatever we say (Matthew 21:21) and if we start to speak out what we want to see come about then we will receive whatever we ask of Him.

In all of this we realise that we have nothing of ourselves. We do not have the ability to heal anyone by our own power or nature; we are totally reliant on God to flow in us and through us by His Holy Spirit. There is nothing we can offer of ourselves that will make us good enough to make that happen. It is God's grace to us that He has given us His Holy Spirit as we could never be holy enough by our own merit. Father God is ever gracious and because He loves us and the people of this world, He will flow through us. When the enemy comes along and says "you are not good enough" just turn around and agree with him. We are not good enough! However, Father's grace *is* sufficient (2 Corinthians 12:9). This, of course, does not mean that we hold back from seeking a deeper relationship with the Lord and we are to be willing to deal with any issues that He highlights in our lives. We must ensure that we respond to the cleansing of the Spirit in order that the flow of His power is not impeded in any way as we seek to minister. We are ever grateful that our anointing is a gift from the Holy Spirit. He has given Himself to us freely because we will never be in a position to deserve such provision through our own human effort.

From this passage we see that having healed this man at the Beautiful Gate, Peter and John start to draw a crowd. This is always an exciting development when we see people healed out on the street. We experienced such an incidence during a mission trip to Bulgaria.

One of our team members, to be honest, was a real pain in the neck! We were having a day off in the middle of a very busy schedule and this did not sit well with him as he thought we should be ministering the whole time we were there. Our hosts were showing us the sights and they took us to visit an Orthodox monastery which some of us found interesting, although not all! Ian was not enjoying himself and wandered off, a regular occurrence with him. The time came to move on and he was nowhere to be found. I searched the area and spotted a crowd of people gathered further down the hill where there were some market stalls set up.

Father said to me, "he's there". I directed the team to get into their cars and to follow me down the hill as I went to fetch our missing friend. Sure enough, there was Ian standing in the middle of the crowd and he is praying for the sick. I asked him, "what on earth are you doing?"

Ian replied, "I'm praying for the sick, Tim" and explains how he was walking through the market because he was bored and God gave him a word of knowledge for a stall keeper. He felt God told him that this lady was suffering from a bad back. She spoke no English and he spoke no Bulgarian but he had managed to relay the fact that God wanted to heal her which I thought was a miracle in itself! He laid hands on her there in the street in front of everyone and she was instantly healed.

A woman managing the adjoining stall saw this happen and there had obviously been quite a commotion because it had taken Ian some time to explain with much waving of hands that God had spoken to him about the first lady's ailment. The second stall keeper had witnessed all of this and said, "I've got a bad hip; will you pray for my hip?" Ian then prayed for her and she too was immediately healed. On my arrival at the scene he had a queue of some twenty-five people wanting prayer. Ian turned to me and asked, "are you having a day off or are you going to do God's will?"

When we start to see miracles of healing on the street then we are going to attract crowds. When Peter and John started to draw a throng who *'were full of amazement'*, Peter got up and made an incredibly bold statement. He challenged the gathered bystanders about their responsibility for the death of Jesus. In our quest for 'user friendly evangelism', our approach would probably take the tack, "oh yes, Jesus has healed this man and He wants to do something for you"! Peter unashamedly grasped the nettle and declared, "you bunch of hypocrites! You killed the Son of God!" He continued on in Acts 3:12 (NAS), *"men or Israel, why are you amazed at this or why do you gaze at us as if by our own power or piety we have made this man walk?"* He explains that while they might have been the disciples that God used to channel His power through, the miracle had little to do with them. We need to realise afresh that no matter how much we have learnt it is God Who heals and all we need to do is to say "yes, Lord, use me".

I consider myself quite fortunate at times that I am not quick enough to ask too many questions of Father. When God says something, I simply endeavour to follow the instruction rather than have a lengthy discussion. I want to encourage you to set your thought processes to one side just enough to be able to hear what He is saying and then to act upon what He tells you to do. Then we will see His power move through us more mightily.

When Peter made this momentous declaration he demonstrated that he understood what Jesus had taught him; to abide in Jesus and allow Him to abide in His followers (John 15:4-11). It is vitally important that we have this two-way relationship with the Lord and that we keep that bond fresh and current. We should not be reliant on our experience of last week, or the beginning of this week, not even on that of yesterday but rather that each moment we seek to abide in Him and allow Him to abide in us in a tangible way. That can be during our quiet time with Him but can also be 'in the moment'. When I am driving in the car, I redeem the time by talking with the Lord. I often seek the Holy Spirit's guidance as He has been sent to *'guide us into all truth'* (John 16:13) especially if I am struggling over some issue. I voice my need, "Holy Spirit, please come and do Your job, I need some help here!" He is gracious to answer as I seek to live in Him and allow Him to live in me. We do well to lean into His Presence wherever we are and so be open to what He is saying.

Jesus taught *'as a branch cannot bear fruit of itself unless it abides in the vine so neither can you unless you abide in Me. I am the vine and you are the branches. He who abides in Me and I in him, he bears much fruit for apart from Me you can do nothing"* (John 15:4-5 NAS). Apart from Jesus we cannot achieve anything of lasting value. We need to position ourselves so that there is an exchange of life between Him and us. The branch abides in the vine. If I cut the branch off on a Sunday evening and take it to work with me and walk around all week with it and then at the end of the week come back the following Sunday and try to tape it back onto the vine, I will not be very successful! I might have to cut out the dead wood. There might just be some small semblance of life evident that I might be able to graft in but it would be difficult because that branch has not abided the whole time; there has been no flow of the life-force, no sap streaming from the vine to the branch and eventually I risk death occurring. If we want to be a people who move in power we need to allow that divine interchange of life to flow from Him to us.

Peter continues, saying *'it was in the Name of Jesus that this man was healed'*. I want to examine this statement. I love the Noel Richards' chorus 'There is power in the Name of Jesus' because there is so much truth in those words. I sing some songs on a Sunday morning and wonder "what on earth is this all about?" I welcome choruses that have life and truth and this particular song we would do well to use as a confession. Here are the lyrics;

> There is power in the Name of Jesus
> We believe in His Name
> We have called on the Name of Jesus
> We are saved, we are saved
> At His Name the demons flee

At His Name captives are free
For there is no other name that is higher than Jesus

There is power in the Name of Jesus
Like a sword in our hands
We declare in the Name of Jesus
We shall stand, we shall stand
At His Name God's enemies
Shall be crushed beneath our feet
For there is no other name that is higher than Jesus

What an awesome confession to make! Get hold of the words and confess it over your life. There is so much truth there. We cannot afford to forget that it is by the Name of Jesus that we are called to minister to those who are oppressed by the devil because there is power in that very Name. When we invoke the Name of Jesus all the weight of heaven comes to back up what we have spoken out and declared in the precious Name of Jesus!

If we take a look through the pages of the New Testament we will discover that there are many times when Jesus tells His followers to act *'in My Name'*. In Mark 16:17 we find one such example; *'and these signs will accompany those who believe, in My Name they will drive out demons, they will speak in new tongues, they will pick up snakes with their hands and when they drink deadly poison it will not hurt them at all. They will place their hands on sick people and they will get well'*.

'In My Name', Jesus declares, you will drive out demons. *'In My Name'* you will speak in tongues. *'In My Name'* you will be able to pick up serpents. *'In My Name'* you will be able to drink poison and it will not harm you. *'In My Name'* you will lay your hands on the sick and they will recover!

A cursory glance through the record of Acts will show that the disciples believed this wholeheartedly and acted upon what Jesus had said to them. Acts 16:17-18 tells us of a slave girl who had been following Paul and crying out, *'these men are the servants of the most high God who are telling you the way of salvation'*. She kept this up for many days until finally Paul became so troubled that he turned and said to the spirit, *'"in the Name of Jesus Christ I command you to come out of her" and at that moment the spirit left her'*. The apostle spoke calmly and with authority. Many ideas have sprung up about what you need to know before delivering a person; the name of the spirit, the reason for its presence, the history of the person involved. Paul simply applied Jesus' teaching, *"in Jesus' Name I command you to come out of this woman"* and we see that she was immediately delivered.

Peter also put this principle into practice when he healed the sick. The apostle declared *'silver and gold I do not have but what I do have I give to you: in the Name of Jesus Christ the Nazarene – walk!'* (Acts 3:6-7). He immediately grabbed the man, pulled him to his feet and the man walked and leaped and praised God, fully restored.

Later when Peter and John are arrested and taken before the Sanhedrin, the apostle declares, *'then know this all you people of Israel - it is by the Name of Jesus Christ of Nazareth Whom you crucified and Whom God raised from the dead – by this Name this man stands before you in good health'* (Acts 4:10 NAS).

There is supremacy in this Name as we move under the power and anointing of the Spirit. On the majority of occasions when I am ministering to the sick, I command health and wholeness *'in the Name of Jesus'* to flow. It is quite clear when you read through the Acts of the Apostles that the early disciples invoked the Name of Jesus when they ministered to those who were in need.

I am reminded of the statement inside the front cover of a British Passport. There it is written; 'Her Britannic Majesty's Secretary of State requests and requires in the name of her Majesty all those to whom it may concern to allow the bearer to pass freely without let or hindrance and to afford the bearer such assistance and protection as may be necessary'. Just how much weight this carries in our modern day society I cannot speculate but my passport has saved my life on at least one occasion.

I was ministering in the war-torn land of Sri Lanka and the Tamil Tigers (a militant organisation seeking their own state in the north of the island) stopped the bus I was traveling on during the curfew. All the passengers were dragged off of the vehicle and I was faced with a young armed teenager. He was very agitated and was pointing his rifle at my chest with much shouting and babbling in a language I could not understand. I very gingerly slid my hand into my top pocket and produced my British passport. Seeing my distinctive blue British passport with the gold crest the guns were lowered and the tension dissipated. Later I was told that if I had pulled out an American or Russian passport the gun would have gone off and I would not have returned home alive. The Tamils historically had worked with the British and held our forefathers in esteem. My British passport had set me free. The guerrillas had respect for the government and authority behind that passport. The enemy of our faith might not have respect for many things, but he does have respect for the authority of God and the Name of Jesus!

Jesus encourages us to use His Name. He did not leave us in any doubt. Our Lord tells us that, *"you did not choose Me but I chose you and appointed you to go and bear fruit, fruit that will last. Then the Father will give you whatever you ask in My Name"* (John 15:16 NAS).

Jesus goes on to say, *"I tell you the truth; My Father will give you whatever you ask in My Name. Until now you have not asked for anything in My Name; ask and you will receive and your joy will be complete"* (John 16:23-24 NAS). I can confirm that this is true because when I have asked God to heal in Jesus' Name, the healing flows and I tell you, I get pretty excited! When you witness Father performing miracles as we declare in Jesus Name that health is returning to people's bodies then you too will be thrilled and your joy will be full!

Again, Jesus declares, *"truly, truly I say to you, he who believes in Me, the works that I do he will do also and greater works than these will he do because I go to the Father. Whatever you ask in My Name that will I do so that My Father may be glorified in the Son. If you ask Me anything in My Name I will do it. If you love Me you will keep My commandments, I will ask the Father and He will give you another helper that He may be with you forever, that is the Spirit of truth Whom the world cannot receive because it does not see Him or know Him but you know Him because He abides with you and will be in you"* (John 14:12-17).

What will believers of Jesus do in His Name? *'These and greater works'*. Jesus promises that we can ask anything in His Name and He will do it. There is no room for doubt as the words He uses are explicit and unambiguous. Jesus declared that the works that He accomplished and even greater works than these, we would do. He stated that we can ask anything. Are there any areas excluded? No because 'anything' is literally anything! He will undertake whatever we ask. This is an incredibly powerful guarantee.

Clearly we need to be abiding in the Vine and it is out of that place that our requests will be the very outcomes that Jesus is looking to see. As we abide so *'we have the mind of Christ'* (1 Corinthians 2:16).

School teachers repeat facts to their students because they wish to emphasise the importance of such truths. When Jesus repeats a principle we would do well to take note! Clearly when we read through the book of Acts there is more involved than just 'naming *the Name of Jesus'* over situations as the cautionary account of the sons of Sceva proves!

'But some of the Jewish exorcists who went from place to place attempted to name over those who had evil spirits the Name of the Lord Jesus saying, "I adjure you by Jesus whom Paul preaches". And seven sons of Sceva, a Jewish chief priest, were doing this. And the evil spirit answered and said to them, "I recognise Jesus and I know about Paul, but who are you?" And the man in whom was the evil spirit, leapt on them and subdued all of them and overpowered them, so that they fled out of the house naked and wounded' (Acts 19:13-16 NAS).

When we come to minister into situations, as we abide in Jesus, we should disappear into the background and it is Jesus Who is at the forefront. Then we will see the power of God released through us. When we call upon His Name all of heaven's resources will be available to us to fulfil whatever we have declared in Jesus' Name. His Name is akin to the signature on a cheque; it validates whatever we specify. It is, of course, conditional on us abiding in Him and having Him abiding in us so that we perceive how the Spirit is working and so the cheque is honoured.

During the time we were planting a church in Bordon I was called out at around one o'clock in the morning to the home of a family who were Christians. They had come along to one of our meetings the previous evening. On their return home the husband had started manifesting in front of his wife and her parents. The situation spiralled out of control and so they phoned me for some help. When I arrived, I rang the doorbell and one of the parents came rushing downstairs, opened the door and beckoned me, "come upstairs quick!" I climbed the stairs to find the other two sitting on top of the husband in the bedroom. He was naked, lying on the floor and spitting a black stream of liquid with such force that it was hitting the ceiling and then dripping back down. He was shouting obscenities and making lewd remarks and his family were thumping him to keep him on the floor.

Our leader Derek had recently been preaching on ministering in the opposite spirit; when we are confronted with anger then we respond from a place of peace. When dealing with demons we do not need to shout, we simply need to speak with the authority we have in God. I remonstrated with the three, "Stop! What on earth are you doing? Get off him now". They obediently jumped to their feet and looked at me as if I were crazy. As the man leapt up I realised that he was wielding a twelve-inch carving knife and he delighted in announcing that he intended to kill me followed by his young children. He bounded across the room and plunged the knife down from above his head towards my chest. I cried out silently, "Lord Jesus, please help me!" The knife stopped four inches from my shirt as if it had hit an invisible barrier. The guy started to shake and the knife dropped out of his hand and suddenly his legs whipped up past my nose as he somersaulted and came to rest on his back on the other side of the room. I delivered him of the demon and calm was restored. I know from my own experience that there is power in the Name of Jesus, bless God!

On another occasion, one of our church members, a 'terribly nice' lady, came along to the midweek meeting with a guest. She sent a message ahead asking, "Tim, will you come downstairs?" She could not persuade the guy to get out of the car and he was making strange noises. Her guest was an alcoholic who lived in a squat near to her home. She had been showing this man the love of Jesus for several months and every day she would take him a hot dinner. To begin with she presented the food on her best china but as she closed the door to leave the squat he would throw the plate at the door. So, rather wisely, she switched to plastic plates! For a whole year she had been taking him food and on each occasion he would hurl the plate after her as she left. Undeterred she returned every day. Eventually he asked her, "why do you keep on doing this?"

"Because Jesus loves you. He has told me to treat you like a son", she replied. She talked with him and he asked if he could come along to a meeting to find out more. On that evening in question he travelled in with her and such was the atmosphere of the Spirit of God in the car that it provoked a reaction. When I arrived the demons within him were manifesting big time!

I opened the back door of the car and he leapt out and crouched on the ground with all the mannerisms of a big cat. He was prowling around the carpark like a panther. I was accompanied by two guys who have not been saved that long and I turned to explain to them, "this is a demon and we are going to cast it out". Our alcoholic friend crawled up to us with a roar and he snarled, "I'm going to eat you!"

I turned to my friends again to reassure them, "don't worry, it's only a demon and we are going to cast it out in Jesus' Name", but they were running in the opposite direction as fast as their legs would carry them! I looked at this man and declared, "in

Jesus' Name I command you to come out" and he was picked up and thrown across the car park and landed fifteen feet away completely delivered.

We do not need to be fearful of demonic activity. The only name we have to know is the Name of Jesus because in His Name there is power and if we are abiding in Him and He in us then we can be confident that He is not going to let anything harmful befall us in this type of situation. When we come across cases of evil possession we can speak to the demons and they will be banished along with sickness, depression and all other products of darkness. They have to leave because there is power in the Name of Jesus.

As the New Testament disciples started to speak in Jesus' Name they saw the power of God released to heal and set people free. Perversely, the authorities objected to them doing so and they were often thrown into prison, flogged and on their release they were commanded not to use the 'Name of Jesus'. I find that interesting. Even today you can speak about the church, you can mention that you are a Christian, you can talk about your Christian friends but when you start to speak about Jesus people often begin to become uneasy and fidgety and may even be rather upset with you. Why? Because there is power in the Name of Jesus. Power to confront and convict. Power to save and to set the captives free. Power to heal those who are sick and tormented by the devil. It is significant that people are uncomfortable when we speak about Jesus. The Holy Spirit is challenging them. So we should not just talk about church, about how nice everyone is, about how wonderful our home group is: rather replace 'church', replace 'home group', replace 'friends' with 'Jesus'. I have a vital relationship with Him and it is important that we let people know that He has changed our lives and that it is this Jesus Who has made such a difference.

We should not be shy about our faith because there are other groups out there that are going for it. Recently a friend was talking to a group of Muslims and they were trying to convert him to Islam. For two and a half hours they unashamedly talked about what their faith meant to them and what a difference it had made in their lives. We have become so politically correct in this country that we hesitate to speak to people about what the truth is, what we have experienced and what has impacted our lives. Where there is a vacuum, voices other than ours will fill the void.

The Muslims informed my friend that there are people converting to Islam wholesale in Britain and they invited him to come and speak to their imam. He went along to meet this prayer leader and was expecting to find somebody of Asian nationality. On looking around the room he was introduced to a man sporting a bushy beard. The imam spoke with a broad Irish accent and explained that he was a convert to Islam. He had been raised in a Catholic school but had turned his back on Christianity and embraced Islam because his new community had unashamedly declared what their faith meant to them. All he had known in his childhood were apologies and reticence rather than a clear declaration of faith.

There is power to set people free in Jesus' Name and we need to proclaim that Name when we connect and converse with others.

Let us follow the early disciples' example and proclaim the Name of Jesus and we will see the burdened set free. We will see demons banished and sickness bow the knee. We will be privileged to perform signs and wonders and even greater acts than Jesus. *'I tell you the truth, anyone who believes in Me will do the same works I have done, and even greater works, because I am going to be with the Father'* (John 14:12). Wow!

If we have put our trust in His salvation and our hope for our future is in Him then we are able to place our confidence in everything that He has said. If Jesus said it then that settles it as far as I am concerned! There is to be no argument. We simply need to bring ourselves into line with the Word and into that place where we are living in Him and He in us (Romans 8:9). Where we will do whatever He says and we will boldly speak in His Name. We should not back off from this position because there is no other name that is higher than the Name of Jesus and *'at the Name of Jesus every knee will bow, of those in heaven, and of those on earth, and of those under the earth'* (Philippians 2:10).

Let us determine to command *in Jesus' Name* that sickness will bow the knee, pain and disabilities will bow the knee, depression will bow the knee, deafness and blindness will bow the knee and cancers will bow the knee.

Father wants us to be a people of power. Will we be that people? Will we pay the price? Will we allow Him to flow in us and will we seek to abide in Him? We will allow His Word to be worked out when we have become a people who do not just believe these principles but actively live them out. A people who are moving in authority and who are anointed with power. Where along with those early disciples we have sought His face and waited *'in the city until you are clothed with power from on high'* (Luke 24:49).

We need to determine to get hold of God and to allow Him to get hold of us!

Chapter Nine

Dealing with Disappointment

I am sure that we have all suffered setbacks to some measure when it comes to the topic of healing. We may have lost people too early in life. There are those who continue to live with chronic conditions that do not appear to show any sign of improvement. Disabilities which limit potential may cast a shadow over lives. In it all, regardless of our prayers and ministry, we may fail to see the breakthroughs that we are looking for. Yet.

I offer the following observations on the subject. It is a brief, personal viewpoint and not intended to be a thorough exegesis of Scripture! I will leave that to far more learned writers. Each of us is treated by Father as unique beings and so our journey is both individual and peculiar to us alone although, of course, we may well share common experiences and responses. Hopefully, my thoughts may be of some value, but if not, I pray that Father will bless you with discovering your answers elsewhere.

Some time ago, I walked out of a clinic having received some less than cheery news, started the car and flicked on the CD player. The opening bars of a Hillsongs number filled the car, 'Jesus, You're all I need, all I need'. In that moment I thought, 'thank You Lord God for the truth of that'.

Comforting though these words are, it is in the working out of that truth that the challenges are encountered.

In earlier pages of this book, we have briefly examined the character of God and Jesus His Son and the many names that He possesses. Simeon, an elderly devout man received the baby Jesus in the Temple and declared, *'Now I can die content for Your promise to me has been fulfilled. With my own eyes I have seen Your Word, the Saviour You sent into the world'* (Luke 2:29:31 TPT). A few verses earlier we read that Simeon was looking for Christ Who is afforded the title of the *'Consolation of Israel'* (Luke 2:25).

Simeon is overwhelmed with emotion that the Word has become flesh. Jesus has come alongside man in the earthly arena and he is able to give thanks and praise as he declares, *'for with my own eyes I have seen Your Salvation'* (Luke 2:30 AMP).

The 'Consolation of Israel' is an Old Testament description of the long-awaited Messiah. And now Simeon sees the active presence of Jesus the Christ coming alongside man.

He is the Christ of consolation. In 2 Corinthians 1:3-4 (AMP), we read that Paul blesses *'the Father of our Lord Jesus Christ, the Father of sympathy, pity and mercy and the God Who is the Source of every comfort, consolation and encouragement. Who comforts us in every trouble, calamity and affliction so that we may in turn be able to comfort and console those who are in any kind of distress with the consolation with which we ourselves have been comforted'.*

The presence of Jesus brings peace and grace, joy and hope and above all else salvation through His death and resurrection. Salvation and consolation go hand in hand and we are able not only to receive His benefits for ourselves but are equipped to minister that same comfort to others as they receive His hope, the healing of their hurts and distress as Jesus brings His mercy to broken hearts and lives. As we come alongside others so we are able to 'be Jesus' to such people who find themselves in difficulty and may even be caught up in tragic circumstances.

Jesus is our Consolation at those times when we need Him most having suffered a letdown or setback.

I think that there is a process we go through when we are faced with discouragement.

Firstly, it is not wrong to grieve when we are disappointed. The Psalmist tells us that *'the Lord is close to the broken hearted and saves those who are crushed of spirit'* (Psalm 34:18). In our conversations with Father God and indeed with each other it is important that we acknowledge our emotions. We are to *'weep with those who weep'* (Romans 12:15) and be a support to each other. Disappointment can leave us angry and resentful. Memories of the event may be at the forefront of our thoughts and even after time has passed may still be there niggling away at the back of our minds. It is valid to allow ourselves time to express those emotions. Both to Father God and to a trusted friend/confidante.

In it all we must make sure that we do not fall into the trap of allowing our dismay to define us. We must not allow it to take us hostage and weigh us down. We must guard against giving such feelings that measure of power. There is an unattributed quote that says, 'don't let today's disappointments cast a shadow over tomorrow's dreams'. It is imperative that we know where our focus is and that we are not knocked off course by our apparent failures. We must be careful not to allow setbacks to shackle us but rather we are to choose to move forward in our journey by holding onto our core values and beliefs.

Hebrews 10:35,39 tells us, *'do not throw away your confidence which has a great reward. You need to persevere so that when you have done the will of God, you will receive what He has promised.... for we are not those who shrink back but rather those who believe'*.

We believe in His plan for us though we may not always understand it fully. Paul tells us that, *'in all things God works for the good of those who love Him'* (Romans 8:28,31) and the apostle goes on to pose the question, *'what then shall we say in response to this? If God has determined to stand with us..........'*.

We must be careful that we are not tempted to lower our sights when we are ministering to the sick. We must ensure that we do not allow our all too painful experiences to water down our beliefs. As Tim will often say, 'disappointments and failures are simply the battle scars of those who are pursuing their God'.

The writer to the Hebrews tells us that we *'do not have a High Priest Who is unable to understand or sympathize with us....*

We can find grace in time of need.... So, let us hold fast our confession of faith in Him' (Hebrews 4:15).

We pray and give thanks. Probably the hardest thing to do! Scripture has much encouragement to give.

- *'Wait for the Lord, be strong, take heart and do not give up'* (Psalm 27:14)

- *'I waited patiently knowing God would come through for me. At last He bent down and listened to my cry. He stooped down to lift me out of danger from the desolate pit I was in. Now He has lifted me up to a firm, secure place and steadied me while I walk along His ascending path'* (Psalm 40:1-2 TPT)

- *'He gives strength to the weary and He increases power to the weak...... those who hope in the Lord will renew their strength and they will soar on the wings of eagles'* (Isaiah 40:29-31)

- *'We are able to do all things through Him Who gives us strength'* (Philippians 4:13)

Disappointment will sap your resolve and cause you to fall into the snare of inactivity. That is the inactivity of not exercising your faith. If the enemy can stop you from ministering to the sick then he has won the day. It is important that we spend time with Father and allow Him to bring His solace and wholeness to us when we have suffered the pain of loss. Allow the Spirit to reaffirm His love, mercy and grace in our lives that we might fully appreciate Him as our Comforter.

We minister from our position of faith. As we allow Father to bring healing to our sorrows, Paul tells us that we are to, *'fix our eyes not on what is seen but on what is unseen'* (2 Corinthians 4:17). Disappointment will have you take your focus away from Jesus and the work of the Kingdom. We need to be prepared to 'go again'. To be single mindedly fixed on the path before us and be prepared to speak out words of faith for *'out of the heart flows the springs of life'* (Proverbs 4:23).

- *'My son, pay attention to what I say, listen closely to My words; do not let them out of your sight, keep them within your heart for they are life to those who find them and health to a man's whole body. Let your eyes look straight ahead and fix your gaze directly before you'* (Proverbs4:20-25 NIV)

- *'Set a guard over my mouth Lord, keep a watch over the door of my lips'* (Psalm 141:3)

Even when times are hardest and we feel our loss the most keenly, we are to keep our eyes fixed on Jesus. Remember the here and now is not the end of the story. Paul reminds us to not lose heart for we are being *'renewed day by day'* (2 Corinthians 4:16). Both Peter and Paul were not men who were strangers to despair and pain. I am sure they were familiar with such questions and doubts that we might have in times of distress. Peter encourages us to, *'prepare our minds for action and set our hope fully on the grace given to us'* (1 Peter 1:13).

How do we prepare our minds? *'Forgetting what lies behind, I strain forward to what lies ahead, to win the prize'* (Philippians 3:13). Paul goes on to say in this chapter that those of you who are spiritually mature and full grown have this kind of mind set. It is important that we do not allow disappointment to hold us back in spiritual infancy. *'Forgetting what is behind'* is to be seen in the context of facing up to the issue of perceived failure, making sure that we are rooted firmly in the fullness of God's love and grace. That we have allowed Him to bind up those wounds with the balm of the Holy Spirit. We seek to fix our eyes on Jesus and be moving forward to see the Kingdom brought near to the lives of others. That they might experience His healing touch and something more of the dynamic of the Kingdom, an experience that makes a difference to their lives.

My prayer is: *'May the Lord Jesus Christ Himself and God our Father Who loved us and by His grace gave us eternal encouragement and good hope, encourage your hearts and strengthen you in every good deed and word'* (2 Thessalonians 2:16).

This is how we deal with disappointment, I would humbly suggest. As we allow Father to build us up and deal with our hurts so we will find that we can go forward and perform those good deeds of healing and bring the words of life to a hurting world.

Chapter Ten

Hindrances to Healing

I want to look at the subject of why people at times do not appear to be healed. Scripture allows for times when we pray for the sick and do not receive the result we had hoped for. We must always be mindful that people suffering from illness need building up and not beating up and come alongside to support, comfort and encourage them in their time of need.

Let us consider what James writes to the twelve tribes which are scattered abroad, *'Is anyone among you suffering? Let him pray. Is anyone cheerful? Let him sing psalms. Is anyone among you sick? Let him call for the elders of the church, and let them pray over him, anointing him with oil in the Name of the Lord. And the **prayer of faith** will save the sick, and the Lord will raise him up. And if he has committed sins, he will be forgiven'* (James 5:13-15 NAS).

James indicates here that if you find yourself suffering from an illness then the first course of action is to pray for yourself. If your prayers are not bringing about your healing then the next step is to call for *'the elders of the church'*, that is, proven men and women of faith who will exercise that faith to bring about the healing you are looking for. When people are sick they are under the attack of the enemy and that can affect their personal level of faith. They may well benefit from having others alongside who will add their measure of faith to see the desired breakthrough.

In my earlier years of moving in faith there were a number of occasions when I fell ill and, having prayed over myself, did not receive my healing. I refused to give up and go to bed for the day. I was a self-employed businessman and if I did not go out to work then there was no income generated. Finding myself in this position I would phone one of the elders of our church and arrange to visit their home to have them pray for me. I would then set off for work declaring that God is faithful to His Word and expecting that truth to be made manifest in my body. Sometimes that happened quickly and by the time I arrived at my first appointment of the day I would be feeling better. On other occasions, there was a battle and it might be a few hours before I started to recover but no matter how long it took I chose to believe that God's Word was and is unwavering.

As we examine some of the reasons why healing is delayed let us always be mindful that they are not to be used as a reproach for the sufferer. This will only serve to push them to despair. We remember the apostle Paul's encouragement to us that when exercising the gifts of the Spirit this must be done in an atmosphere of love and support. *'But now abide faith, hope, love, these three; but the greatest of these is love'* (1 Corinthians 13:13 NAS).

As we seek to minister to the sick we need to operate in love and be motivated by compassion. The unwell are not notches to be added to our spiritual reputation or failures to be blamed and cast aside when our faith does not prevail. They are people who have been oppressed by the enemy and need to experience the victory that Jesus has won for us all.

Before we reflect on some of the reasons why people do not experience God's healing power let us be clear that there is no deficiency on the part of Father God. Having purchased our healing through the sacrifice of His Son it is inconceivable that He would now want to withhold such provision from us. The prophet Isaiah, some seven hundred years before the birth of the Messiah, looked forward to the day when Jesus would accomplish all this and declared that *'by His stripes we are healed'* (Isaiah 53:5). Not we might be, not we can be, but *'we **are** healed'*. Jesus' atonement was a complete work.

It is often recorded that when Jesus met the sick He was moved with compassion and healed them all (Matthew 14:14). Empathy motivated Him to go out of His way to help the physical, spiritual and emotional needs of the people that He met as He travelled through His earthly ministry. Logically, if there is no deficiency on His part then we must conclude that the shortcoming may be found in us. That is an uncomfortable truth for us to acknowledge but it should inspire us to a deeper relationship with Father that we might be able to address the deficit.

There are only a couple of times recorded in the gospels where people were not immediately totally healed and both of those incidences are worth taking a look at. There are lessons to be gleaned.

'.... they came to Bethsaida. And they brought a blind man to Jesus and implored Him to touch him. Taking the blind man by the hand, He brought him out of the village; and after spitting on his eyes and laying His hands on him, He asked him, "Do you see anything?" And he looked up and said, "I see men, for I see them like trees, walking around." Then again He laid His hands on his eyes; and he looked intently and was restored and began to see everything clearly. And He sent him to his home, saying, "Do not even enter the village' (Mark 8:22-26 NAS).

We can see here that Jesus worked a wonderful miracle. He did not pray for the man but rather He spat in his eyes and laid His hands on him. Jesus then asked him what he could see. There was some immediate improvement but the man still could not see clearly. Note that Jesus was not disappointed and that He did not settle for the partial improvement. He laid His hands on the man's eyes again and we are told the man looked intently and began to see clearly.

When we are ministering to the sick we need to be open to the leading of the Spirit. There may well be some action that is required on our part or indeed something the person you are ministering to needs to do. Jesus spat in the man's eyes before laying His hands upon him after which he began to see. When it was apparent that he still was not seeing perfectly then Jesus laid His hands on him a second time. The man looked carefully and he began to see clearly. When we are ministering to the sick we are not to rely on formulas but rather we are to be open to the leading of the Holy Spirit and willing to act on His instruction.

Jesus took the man out of the village. Some commentators say that He did so to remove him from an atmosphere of unbelief. Perhaps that was why the man did not receive complete healing immediately. It is possible that the hangover of unbelief was still about him and Jesus was compelled to minister a second time. This is purely conjecture but it is safe to say that Jesus changed the environment for a reason that no doubt Father God had revealed to Him. When Jesus spat in the man's eyes and laid His hands on him, Jesus was expecting something to change as evidenced by His question. Jesus persisted until He saw the miracle completed.

The second account I want to look at is found in Mark 9. A father brought his son to the disciples and they ministered to him but were not able to deliver him from what oppressed him. The boy's father was clearly not satisfied with the outcome and so he pushed through to Jesus Who then delivered the boy from the spirit that was troubling him.

It is useful to note how the disciples reacted to this turn of events. They did not make a doctrine based on their own short comings and failures as many try to do. They did not allow their experience to dictate what they believed rather than God's Word. Instead they came to Jesus privately and asked, *'why couldn't we drive it out?'* He explained to them what the problem was and how to overcome it for another time.

Lack of success is not the lynchpin to build our beliefs and doctrines around. It is a place from which we return to our Master to learn how we might succeed the next time we find ourselves in the same position.

Jesus called the disciples part of an *'unbelieving (faithless) generation'* (Mark 9:19). Here is exampled one reason why people fail to be healed. That is;

- **Unbelief**

    Unbelief can be manifest in both those ministering and those who are sick.

As we have seen, Jesus told the disciples when they could not cast out the demon that it was due to their unbelief. The gospel of Matthew records that it was *'because you have so little faith'* (Matthew 17:20 NAS). The presence of unbelief will restrict the success of our faith.

The Lord went on to tell them that *'however, this kind does not go out except by prayer and fasting'* (Matthew 17:21 NAS).

I have come to realise that it is the unbelief for a given situation that we are to be delivered from by engaging in prayer and fasting. We are to set aside time that we spend in taking on board nutrition to feed our spirits by developing our relationship with Father. The subsequent release of faith in Jesus will overcome all that is set before us. *'You can say to this mountain, 'Move from here to there' and it will move. Nothing will be impossible for you'* (Matthew 17:20 NAS). Whether that be a physical mountain, emotional or spiritual.

Jesus encourages us that it is by disciplining our bodies and our natural appetites that we may use the time that releases to spend with God. As we go deeper with Him so unbelief is expelled. We read that when Jesus came out of the wilderness after forty days of prayer and fasting, *'when the devil had finished every temptation, he left Him until a more opportune time. Then Jesus returned* **in the** *power of the Spirit to Galilee, and news of Him went out through all the surrounding region'* (Luke 4:13-14 NAS).

Spending time in fellowship with God empowers us to overcome the devil's temptations, one of which is to doubt our identity as a full son and heir of the Kingdom and that all power and authority is ours. That unbelief is dispelled enabling us to return from the wilderness in the power of the Holy Spirit just as Jesus did. Prayer and fasting enables us to banish unbelief from our hearts.

Unbelief can also work in those around us. When Jesus visited His hometown we are told that, *'He did not do many miracles there because of their unbelief'* (Matthew 13:58 NAS).

Mark's gospel tells us that, *'He could do no miracle there except that He laid His hands on a few sick people and healed them. And He wondered at their unbelief'* (Mark 6:5-6 NAS).

There is no doubt that Jesus was full of the Holy Spirit and moved entirely in the power that came from that anointing. Yet unbelief in the people limited what Jesus was able to do among them. Interestingly we note that it did not stop Him moving in power completely as reported by both Matthew and Mark!

As far as is possible we need to deal with unbelief in ourselves and seek to build faith in those we are ministering to. We recognise that we are responsible for the former while we understand that the latter is a process that may take some time. We should always come alongside people and seek to move them on in their journey of faith as far as is possible.

- **Unconfessed sin**

….. can certainly be a blockage to God's healing power in our lives. Revisiting James 5:16 (NAS) we find him encouraging the Jewish brethren to, *'confess your sins to each other and pray for each other so that you may be healed. The prayer of a righteous man is powerful and effective'*.

Clearly, hidden sin can restrict healing from flowing and it can also be the foothold that allows the enemy to introduce sickness into our lives. We see this attested to in the story set at the Pool of Bethesda.

'Now a certain man was there who had an infirmity thirty-eight years. When Jesus saw him lying there, and knew that he already had been in that condition a long time, He said to him, "Do you want to be made well?" The sick man answered Him, "Sir, I have no man to put me into the pool when the water is stirred up; but while I am coming, another

steps down before me". Jesus said to him, "Rise, take up your bed and walk"' (John 5:5-8 AMP).

Further on in the account we read that, '*A short time later, Jesus found the man at the temple, and said to him, "Look at you now! You're healed! Walk away from your sin so that nothing worse will happen to you"*' (John 5:14 TPT).

Jesus connected this man's sin with his sickness and encouraged him to actively repent and turn away from any wrongdoing that would seek to ensnare him again. If we continually refuse to deal with sin in our lives then we may well suffer the consequences. Wilfully stepping out from under the covering of the Covenant means that we are flirting with the possibility that the enemy will be free to attack us. We are cautioned that, '*an undeserved curse will be powerless to harm you. It may flutter over you like a bird, but it will find no place to land*' (Proverbs 26:2 TPT).

King David lamented, '*now my body is sick. My health is totally broken because of Your anger and it's all due to my sins!*' (Psalm 38:3 TPT). A cautionary tale that there can be consequences to unconfessed sin which may manifest in our bodies as sickness or disease. However, we need to be mindful not to blame every sickness on sin; it is but one possible reason for illness. Walking openly and honestly before Father will allow the Spirit to highlight any issues that may be in our lives. We can confidently come to Father to deal with any such areas. If we are unaware of any problems then resist looking for 'reds under the bed' and move on.

- **Unforgiveness**

…. can hinder healing. Jesus taught, *'therefore I say to you, whatever things you ask when you pray, believe that you receive them, and you will have them. And whenever you stand praying, if you have anything against anyone, forgive him, that your Father in heaven may also forgive you your trespasses. But if you do not forgive, neither will your Father in heaven forgive your trespasses'* (Mark 11:24-26 NAS).

Christ links answered prayer with our willingness to forgive others. If we hold onto resentment rather than dealing with an issue a blockage is created restricting the release of answers to our requests of Father God. When such a request concerns healing we may well not see the outcome we want.

Corrie Ten Boon wrote, 'unforgiveness is like drinking poison and expecting the other person to die!' It will have a devastating effect. There is some medical evidence that indicates that attitudes such as harbouring unforgiveness can affect the chemical makeup of our bodies. This results in them becoming a more hostile environment for good health. Such conditions as arthritis thrive in a body at war with itself. I am not asserting that all arthritis is caused by unforgiveness but it would appear that there is a credible indication that there are natural consequences to unforgiveness.

My experience tells me that if unforgiveness or sin is the trigger behind an illness then more often than not the sick person is aware that they are struggling in a particular area of their life. They require help and consideration rather than condemnation and should be respectfully encouraged to search their heart and be open and honest about any failings so that they might be dealt with.

I have experienced this in my own life as I have shared in an earlier chapter. This has allowed me to be sensitive when this is a problem in the lives of those I am ministering to. This was particularly brought home to me a number of years ago while I was on mission in Sri Lanka.

At the end of one of the meetings I was praying for the sick when up came a gentleman with a very obviously withered hand.

Myself and Charles (a gifted friend who was travelling

with me) laid our hands on this guy and commanded healing. Miraculously, the arm untwisted and straightened out. Outstanding. There was much rejoicing!

Several minutes later, suddenly the arm twisted again and we were back to square one. Well, we were not standing for that so we prayed a second time. The arm straightened out but again several minutes later it twisted once more.

So, undeterred, we went again for a third time but the same sequence of events happened once more. The penny finally dropped that maybe something more was going on which was preventing the healing from 'sticking'.

I spent time talking through with the guy who told me that when his father had died some years ago, the will had divided up the farmland between the three sons. This guy's portion, in his opinion, was not as good as the other plots and he tried to negotiate with his brothers for a more equitable distribution of the land. The brothers refused and wanted to stay with the stipulation of the will.

This man told me that he was terribly upset by this and because his brothers needed access through his land to reach their plots, he refused permission for them to cross his land. He could not bring himself to forgive his brothers for acting, in his eyes, unfairly towards him.

I explained to this guy that I was sure that it was this very attitude of unforgiveness which meant his arm could not be healed. Would he rather not forgive and have his arm restored? He had seen with his own eyes what that would mean. Sadly, he just could not let go of the animosity he felt for his family and left the meeting still with his withered arm.

A sobering story of how unforgiveness blocks healing. If unforgiveness is present you can have all the faith in the world but that hardness of heart will undo the work of faith every time.

You see, the work of the Cross in our lives flows in two directions. The great teacher Derek Prince points us to the structure of the Cross. It is made up of two pieces of wood; a vertical and a horizontal bar.

Forgiveness comes vertically from God when we acknowledge Jesus' sacrifice for us. Forgiveness must also flow horizontally from one believer to another. If it does not, the vertical flow will be dammed up and forgiveness of our sins will cease. An extremely dangerous place to find ourselves. Let us all keep short accounts and make sure that we are walking in unity together with no unresolved issues.

- **Lack of teaching or poor understanding**

.... can handicap healing. The Lord God says, *'My people are destroyed for lack of knowledge'* (Hosea 4:6).

On a number of occasions I have ministered to people who are convinced that Father God Himself has put sickness upon them in order to teach them a lesson and make them a 'better Christian'. I cannot possibly imagine that a loving Father would deliberately make their child sick in order to teach that child a lesson!

'Every good and perfect gift is from above, coming down from the Father of the heavenly lights, Who does not change like shifting shadows' (James 1:17).

I do not ever imagine that sickness is good or perfect as God declares Himself to be a healing God and He does not change His mind.

Once when discussing this miscomprehension with someone who was certain that Father had made them ill so they could be taught something more in God, I asked them if they were taking any medication for the sickness. They told me they were under the direction of their doctor and were taking a course of pills.

So, extrapolating their line of reasoning to its natural conclusion, I suggested that by doing this they were in rebellion to God and they should immediately stop taking the medicine and learn the lesson quickly so that they might be healed. As you can imagine they were more than a little indignant by this observation and asked me if I was mad!

I replied in the negative but tentatively suggested that I thought they were deceived if they believed that a Father Who declares Himself to be the God Who heals us, Who sent His only Son into this world to be scourged that we might be made whole would then use sickness to teach us a lesson.

Poor teaching and a lack of understanding can prevent people pursuing and receiving their healing.

'For the ways of a man are before the eyes of the Lord, And He watches all his paths. He will die for lack of instruction' (Proverbs 5:21,23 NAS).

'The lips of the righteous feed many, but fools die for lack of understanding' (Proverbs 10:21 NAS).

Isaiah 53:5 clearly declares that *'by His wounds we are healed'*. It has already been done and all we have to do is to receive our healing by faith in the same way in which we received our salvation.

- **Pride**

    …. can be a stumbling block. When we think we know better than God! In 2 Kings 5:10-14 (NAS) we find the account of Naaman who came to the prophet in Samaria seeking healing from his leprosy.

    'Elisha sent a messenger to him, saying, "Go and wash in the Jordan seven times, and your flesh will be restored to you and you will be clean". But Naaman was furious and went away and said, "Behold, I thought, 'He will surely come out to me and stand and call on the name of the Lord his God and wave his hand over the place and cure the leper'. Are not Abanah and Pharpar, the rivers of Damascus, better than all the waters of Israel? May I not wash in them and be clean?" So he turned and went away in a rage'.

    Naaman was too proud to take the course of action that God had directed.

- **Lack of Discernment**

    'For anyone who eats and drinks without discriminating and recognizing with due appreciation that it is Christ's body, eats and drinks a sentence (a verdict of judgement) upon himself. That careless and unworthy participation is the

reason many of you are weak and sickly, and quite enough of you have fallen into the sleep of death. For if we would judge ourselves, we would not be judged' (1 Corinthians 11:29-31 AMP).

Clearly there were problems in the Corinthian church. Paul perceived that there were divisions and factions among the people and they were neglectful of caring for one another. Some were eating and drinking and were even getting drunk while others in the church were going hungry.

Paul tells them that because of this lack of sensitivity towards the Lord's Body many were suffering from illness and some had even succumbed to disease. The apostle encouraged them that prior to coming to the communion table they should take time to examine themselves and their attitudes towards each other. They should ensure that they were reflecting Christ's nature one to another and if they should find themselves lacking to seek to put things right. In this way they would avoid bringing judgement upon themselves.

We would do well to apply the same principles of discernment today in our church life.

- **Poor state of mind or spirit**

    …. as illustrated in a number of Scriptures that point to the fact that the condition of our mind and spirit can have an effect on our bodies well-being.

    'A happy heart is good medicine and a cheerful mind works healing, but a broken spirit dries up the bones' (Proverbs 17:22 AMP).

    'The spirit of a man will sustain him in sickness, But who can bear a broken spirit?' (Proverbs 18:14).

    'Hope deferred makes the heart sick, but a longing fulfilled is a tree of life' (Proverbs 13:12).

    Jesus predicted that in the end times, *'men's hearts will fail them from fear and the expectation of those things which are coming on the earth ….'* (Luke 21:26 NAS).

    Sometimes people fail to be healed because of trauma and wounds from their past which impinge on their capacity to receive. They might well benefit from receiving emotional or spiritual support before they can embrace physical healing. The prophet Isaiah declares, *'the Spirit of the Lord God is upon Me, because the Lord has anointed Me to preach good tidings to the poor; He has sent Me to heal the broken hearted, to proclaim liberty to the captives, and the opening of the prison to those who are bound; to proclaim the acceptable year of the Lord, and the day of vengeance of our God; to comfort all who mourn, to console those who mourn in Zion, to give them beauty for ashes, the oil of joy for mourning, the garment of praise for the spirit of heaviness'* (Isaiah 61:1-3).

Clearly our physical body responds to our state of mind and spirit. Jesus came to remedy this situation and break the strongholds that such emotions can inflict on us.

- **Demonic activity**

…. can restrict healing from flowing freely. When Jesus called His twelve disciples together, He *'gave them power and authority over all demons, and to heal diseases'* (Luke 9:1 NAS).

Demons not only cause sickness but they can also hinder healing. In certain situations it is not just a matter of ministering healing to the sick person. We must cast out or bind the forces which are instrumental in oppressing the person with disease.

Examples of this are the;

spirit of infirmity ~ Luke 13:10-11
spirit of epilepsy ~ Matthew 17:14-15
spirit of depression ~ Isaiah 61:3
deaf and dumb spirit ~ Mark 9:14-29
spirit of blindness ~ Matthew 12:22

Peter identified sickness as harassment or oppression by the power of the devil (Acts 10:38).

As I have already written, it amazes me how when I have begun to bind the spirits behind a sickness just how many times demonic activity has been manifested. Deliverance from those forces of darkness have resulted in freedom from sickness and disease.

- **Weak confession**

'Look at the ships, though they are so great and are driven by strong winds, they are still directed by a very small rudder wherever the inclination of the pilot desires. So also the tongue is a small part of the body, and yet it boasts of great things. See how great a forest is set aflame by such a small fire! And the tongue is a fire, the very world of iniquity; the tongue is set among our members as that which defiles the entire body,

and sets on fire the course of our life, and is set on fire by hell' (James 3:4-6 NAS).

James instructs us that our tongue controls the course of our lives and has the ability to pollute our entire body. From the same mouth can come both blessing and cursing (verse 9) and even *'death and life are in the power of the tongue....'* (Proverbs 18:21 NAS).

We need to be careful of what we say! If we continually confess negatives over our lives we should not be surprised when undesirable events befall us.

Statements such as, "well, this condition runs in my family; my mother had it so I expect I will suffer with it as well" and "I know that I've been prayed for but that never works for me so I'm not expecting to get better".

Why would we want to speak such damaging words over our lives? It is far better to confess God's Word and what He says about our situation! Father says, *'My son, give attention to My words; Incline your ear to My sayings. Do not let them depart from your eyes; Keep them in the midst of your heart; For they are life to those who find them, And health to all their flesh'* (Proverbs 4:20-22 NAS).

Our words have power! Jesus encourages us, *'have faith in God. Truly I say to you, whoever says to this mountain, 'Be taken up and cast into the sea,' and does not doubt in his heart, but believes that what he says is going to happen, it will be granted to him'* (Mark 11:22-23 NAS).

This is a double edged promise! If we believe that the words that come from our mouth will become reality then we will not be disappointed. Therefore, let us be mindful of what we say so as to steer a constructive course for our lives.

Let us also be a people who speak words of encouragement and communicate blessing and healing on those we come across who are sick.

As we seek to address any of the above issues that may occur in our lives we can be confident that we are putting ourselves in the position of being clear channels through which the Holy Spirit can flow to work miracles of healing in both our own lives as well as those of others.

CHAPTER ELEVEN

Full of the Holy Spirit

It is essential to be a people full of the Holy Spirit if we are to be anointed with power and moving in the ministry of healing. We must daily be looking to see the Spirit flowing in us and through us to others. I am reminded of the book 'Good Morning, Holy Spirit' by the evangelist Benny Hinn. These are the first words to come out of his mouth on wakening each new day. We would do well to ask the Spirit each morning, "How can I cooperate with You today?"

There must be an awareness of continual fellowship with the third Person of the Trinity and a desire to develop our relationship with Him (2 Corinthians 13:14). Father's purpose is to create a community of believers who are bound to Him in the covenant relationship that is encapsulated by the words, *'I will be your God and you will be My people'* (Leviticus 26:12). The Spirit initiates new believers into the church, transforms our lives, seals our salvation, gives gifts to help us serve the body, fosters our worship and reminds us of Christ.

We are to be submitted to the leading and guidance of the Spirit. We recognise that He is a Person Who chooses to interact with us and as such can be;

- Grieved ~ The Spirit is a Person Who is sensitive and can be hurt by our behaviour and attitudes.

  As the Spirit lives in us any of our actions which are not under His control have the potential to bring anguish to Him. We are not to limit His scope or access to our lives but be mindful that, *'The Holy Spirit of God has sealed you in Jesus Christ until you experience your full salvation. So never grieve the Spirit of God or take for granted His holy influence in your life'* (Ephesians 4:30 TPT).

- Stifled ~ We are to be committed to a way of life that is Spirit led. Let us not subdue the gifts (which, of course, healing is one such) as this impoverishes the church. We should encourage the work of the Spirit in everyone's lives and support the full expression of the gifts to benefit mankind. *'Never restrain or put out the fire of the Holy Spirit'* (1 Thessalonians 5:19 TPT).

- Resisted ~ *'Why would you be so stubborn as to close your hearts and ears to me? You are always opposing the Holy Spirit, just like your fathers of old did before you!'* (Acts 7:51 TPT).
  Stephen took the Sanhedrin, the supreme council, to task for rejecting God's leaders and the Messiah. If we refuse to follow Father's direction for our lives which has been given to us through His Word and His Holy Spirit then we are in danger of resisting His influence and work in us.

- Insulted ~ We are asked, *'How much more severely do you suppose a person deserves to be judged who has contempt for God's Son, and who scorns the blood of the new covenant that made him holy, and who mocks the Spirit of grace?'* (Hebrews 10:29 TPT). We should give serious consideration to this warning.

- Blasphemed ~ *'This is why I warn you, for God, will forgive people for every sin and blasphemy they have committed except one. There is no forgiveness for the sin of blasphemy against the Holy Spirit'* (Matthew 12:31-32 TPT).

Jesus confronted the Pharisees who had attributed the power by which He performed miracles to Satan rather than the Holy Spirit (verse 24). The 'unpardonable sin' is the considered refusal to acknowledge God's power in Christ. It displays a deliberate and irreversible hardness of the heart. If a person should reject the conviction of the Holy Spirit then they distance themselves from the only agent in their lives Who can lead them to repentance and restoration to God.

- Lied to ~ *'God revealed their secret to Peter so he said to him, "Ananias, why did you let Satan fill your heart and make you think you could lie to the Holy Spirit?"'* (Acts 5:3 TPT). Even after the Holy Spirit has come we are not immune to Satan's temptations. Although the enemy was defeated at the Cross he is still actively enticing believers to stumble (Ephesians 6:12, 1 Peter 5:8). Ananias and Sapphira's sin was lying to both the Spirit and God's people. Dishonesty, greed and self-promotion are toxic in the church environment and prevent the Holy Spirit from working effectively. Let us, *'put on God's complete set of armour provided for us, so that we will be protected as we fight against the evil strategies of the accuser!'* (Ephesians 6:11 TPT).

- Rebelled against ~ *'Yet they rebelled and grieved His Holy Spirit'* (Isaiah 63:10). The Holy Spirit attempts to guide our lives to Godly actions. When we rebel we choose to follow our own desires and resist the Spirit which pains Father God. Rebellious Christians need to consider the Cross of Christ afresh and remember God's grace on their lives. This should lead to repentance and renewal of their commitment. Only then is the Spirit able to bring rest, redemption and peace to our hearts.

We need to ensure that we give the Holy Spirit the same respect, honour and place in our lives that we give to God our Father and His Son Jesus Christ. We should seek to continually draw from the Spirit and allow Him to flow in us and through us.

Jesus made this clear when He prophesied about the coming Holy Spirit.

'Then on the most important day of the feast, the last day, Jesus stood and cried out, saying, "If anyone is thirsty, let him come to Me and drink. He who believes in Me, as the Scripture said, from his innermost being will flow rivers of living water". Jesus was prophesying about the Holy Spirit that believers were being prepared to receive...' (John 7:37-39 NAS).

Accepting Christ means that we receive Him as the 'Water of Life' (John 4:10). Believers live in Christ much like fish live in water: He is to be our natural element!

Here Jesus is bringing two images together, that of life (John 6:63) and water (John 3:5). Whoever believes in Jesus will be baptized in the Spirit as prophesied by John the Baptist (John 1:33).

The Greek for *'come'* (verse 37) implies frequent drinking so we should read, *'if anyone is thirsty let him keep coming and keep drinking'*. Likewise Paul writes in the present continuous tense to, *'be being filled with the Holy Spirit'* (Ephesians 5:18).

Jesus intends that the experience of being saturated with the Holy Spirit is to be a continuous occurrence. It involves a choice on our part that is dependent upon an ongoing yearning and a desire to satisfy that craving by coming and drinking.

We simply have to ask. *'If imperfect parents know how to lovingly take care of their children and give them what they need, how much more will the perfect heavenly Father give the Holy Spirit's fullness when His children ask Him'* (Luke 11:13 TPT).

What is it that creates this desire within us?

Firstly it is essential that we recognise our need of the Holy Spirit. We know the account of Jesus interacting with the Samaritan woman at the well (John 4:13-14 TPT) and instructing her that, *'If you drink from Jacob's well you'll be thirsty again and again, but if anyone drinks the living water I give them, they will never thirst again and will be forever satisfied! For when you drink the water I give you it becomes a gushing fountain of the Holy Spirit, springing up and flooding you with endless life!'*

Secondly we must acknowledge what Jesus tells His disciples, *'here's the truth: it's to your advantage that I go away, for if I do not go away the Divine Encourager will not be released to you; but if I go I will send Him to you'* (John 16:7 TPT).

I sympathise with these followers who found it difficult to comprehend that anything could be better than having Jesus living with them in the here and now! Yet He tells the disciples that it is to their benefit that He leaves them. Of course, His subsequent death and resurrection bringing eternal salvation along with the infilling of the Spirit bore that out!

What does the Holy Spirit seek to bring to our lives?

*'But when the Father sends the **Helper**, the One like Me Who sets you free, He will **teach** you all things in My Name. And He will inspire you to **remember** every word that I've told you'* (John 14:26).

*'But when He, the Spirit of truth comes, He will **unveil the reality of every truth within you**. He will not speak on His own initiative, but only what He hears from the Father, and He will **reveal prophetically to you what is to come**. He will glorify Me on the earth, for He will receive from Me what is Mine and reveal it to you'* (John 16:13-14 TPT).

Jesus promised the disciples that the Holy Spirit would help by reminding them of what He had taught them. The disciples were eye-witnesses of Jesus' life and teachings and the Spirit aided them in their recall without detracting from their individual perspectives. We can be confident that the Gospels are accurate accounts. The Spirit can help us in the same way. As we study the Word we can trust Him to plant truth in our minds and reveal Father's will to us.

Furthermore, we are to have a thirst for more of the Spirit as we recognise the need of the world. *'"Not by might nor by power, but by My Spirit," says the Lord Almighty'* (Zechariah 4:6).

When we see the immense lack within humanity and accept the Great Commission (Matthew 28:19) we might well be overwhelmed with feelings of inadequacy. The needs of this world are simply too great for us to address on our own. The presence of the Holy Spirit is essential for us to fulfil the Lord's assignment and that realisation must fuel our thirst for more of Him working and moving through us.

On our own we have neither the ability nor power to fulfil God's plans. Father chooses to work through us. Our efforts alone will achieve little. It is only though the Spirit that anything of lasting value is accomplished. We should determine to not solely trust our own strength or ability but rather we should depend on the Spirit and co-labour with His power.

The Holy Spirit partners with us to reach a lost world.

Jesus told the disciples, *'When the Spirit comes He will convince the world of its sin, and of the availability of God's goodness, and of deliverance from judgement'* (John 16:8).

So often people in the world mistakenly feel that the church condemns them for their shortcomings when actually God is giving folk the opportunity to be set free from their sin. The truth of *'this is how much God loved the world ~ He gave His one and only unique Son as a gift. So now everyone who believes in Him will never perish but experience everlasting life'* (John 3:16 TPT) is paramount to our faith.

The Holy Spirit was sent to persuade people of their need, not to condemn them but rather to convince them of the availability of God's deliverance (John 16:8). We need the Spirit to work among the people of this world in preparation for us to speak into their lives and point them to salvation.

What is it we are empowered to do?

Jesus promised the disciples, *'I will send the fulfilment of the Father's promise to you. So stay in the city until you are anointed with power from on high that wraps around you'* (Luke 24:49 TPT).

We are destined to be a people who are clad with power in all its fullness. We are to allow the Holy Spirit unrestricted access to our lives.

The Spirit came that we might be anointed with power so that we can **preach the good news** effectively accompanied by a demonstration of His supreme strength.

'Jesus said to them, "As you go into all the world, preach openly the wonderful news of the Gospel to the entire human race! Whoever believes the good news and is baptized will be saved and whoever does not believe the good news will be condemned. And these miracle signs will accompany those who believe; they will drive out demons in the power of My Name. They will speak in tongues. They will be supernaturally protected from snakes and from drinking anything

poisonous. And they will lay hands on the sick and heal them"' (Mark 16:15-18 TPT).

These signs are to accompany *'those who believe'*. It is not just for the super saints if such a thing exists! It is for every follower to move in the power of the Holy Spirit. We are to;

- preach the gospel to all creation
- have authority over demons
- speak in languages not known to us
- move under the protection of our Lord
- heal the sick (which should include raising the dead)

We look to Jesus for our lead;

*'The Spirit of the Lord is upon Me and He has **anointed** Me to be the **hope** of the poor, **freedom** for the broken hearted, and **new eyes** for the blind, and to **preach** to prisoners, 'You are set free!' I have come to share the message of Jubilee for the time of God's **great favour** has begun ...... These Scriptures came true today in front of you'* (Luke 4:18-19, 21 TPT).

Just as our Lord recognised that He was anointed by the Holy Spirit to carry out all His God appointed tasks, how much more do we have need of the constant infilling of the Spirit? We cannot operate on our own and we cannot function on yesterday's measure of anointing. It is essential that we are filled and are being filled continuously each day with the Spirit.

Jesus was clear in His anointing of the Spirit and proved it throughout His walk on earth. Especially when ministering to the sick;

'The power of the Lord was present for Him to heal the sick' (Luke 5:17).

'All the people were trying to touch Him for power was coming from Him and healing them all' (Luke 6:19 NAS).

'Jesus said, "someone did touch Me for I was aware that power had gone out of Me"' (Luke 8:46 NAS).

If we are to be the people of power that Jesus anticipates us to be it is imperative that we seek to be constantly filled with the Holy Spirit and let the river of life flow out from us to those around (Ezekiel 47:12).

Let us remember Jesus' words; *"if anyone is thirsty let him keep coming and keep drinking from Me"*.

Are you thirsty?

CHAPTER TWELVE

Guidelines for Ministry

When ministering to people outside of the church family there are certain strategies and courtesies that we have found to be helpful.

These guidelines have been developed over our many years of ministering to the sick and are designed to put people at ease to receive a touch from the Lord.

If you are ministering within the environment of your church building, it is vitally important that you are incredibly welcoming. When people set foot in your building do not leave them hovering at the door. Sounds obvious but it is good to realise that when someone arrives they may well be a little unsure about what to do next so please try to put them at their ease. Make sure they feel comfortable, say 'hello' to them and draw them in, perhaps introduce them to someone else. It may well be the first time in many years that they have set foot across the threshold of a church building and they may not be too sure about what to expect. Do not worry that you are being 'over the top', you really will not be! Make them feel at home. So, as to the guidelines;

- When praying **as far as possible pray with one or two others**. This brings the power of agreement to your prayers (Matthew 18:19). It also means that you will not be in a vulnerable position. When Jesus sent the disciples out He sent them in pairs and told them to be as *'wise as serpents'* (Matthew 10:16). That advice still holds good today. When praying with people we might not be privy to their background, we do not know what agenda they may have so the 'safety in numbers' approach is a good principle. This means we are above reproach and importantly, it will help to allay any concerns the person we are ministering to may have. Generally, people will be much more comfortable with two or three people praying for them than perhaps a 'one on one' approach. Of course, so importantly, it is in the power of agreement that authority is released as we minister.

- Recognise that it is best for just one to **take the lead** in speaking to the person being ministered to and all comments should then be made through that leader as far as is possible. We have found that it is important that the person leading the prayer is sympathetic and those receiving ministry only have a single voice addressing them.

- Always **ask** what they particularly want prayer for. Never make assumptions even if you think it seems obvious. We had a friend who had suffered from a badly deformed spine since birth which had left her quite hunched over. She would go forward at any opportunity at a healing service and guess what people prayed for? The deformed spine. When we spoke to her she actually did not request prayer for her physical problem but rather was deeply in need of emotional healing for hurts that she had suffered in the past. People mistakenly assumed that she wanted healing for her spine. It is an old saying, I know, but if we assume then we can make an 'ass out of u and me' and that is to be avoided at all costs! So please do not presume that you know what the person would like prayer for.

- Never **pray for a minor** without a parent or guardian present and always seek to help the child to understand what is going on. There are a few basic common sense steps that you can put in place. Ask them to tell you what they thought you said. It can be quite illuminating! Especially if you are out of the habit of dealing with younger children and using age appropriate language. When you are speaking with children always make sure that you come down to their level physically so that you can engage eye to eye. Small children can find it quite intimidating if you are looking down at them.

Guidelines for Ministry

- Take the time to **explain to those you are ministering to** how you are going to pray and what that involves. Briefly read or quote any relevant Scriptures. It is important to take the mystery out of the process. Remember this may be a completely new experience for them. Share with them simply what the Bible teaches. Tell them that when we lay our hands on the sick they will recover and quote whichever Scripture you feel is pertinent to their situation. It is all about making them comfortable with the process so they may be confident to receive.

- When ministering, it's always good to **ask God** how you should minister and agree this together with anyone else who is ministering with you. Explain to the person you are ministering to that you are actually going to take a moment to ask God how He wants you to pray for them. Every situation is different; they are unique and God knows exactly how He is going to move in their life. Avoid taking more than a minute to do this otherwise they may begin to feel rather nervous. Take input from any others ministering with you and decide which direction to take and the manner in which you will pray. If you are ministering with someone else and your sense of what Father is directing is put to one side by them do not be tempted to question them in front of the person being ministered to. By all means have a discussion after the session but remember it is unity that is important and the person being ministered to does not need to be confused by having somebody say 'well, hang on a minute…..'

- While you are praying **be open to God** revealing the root cause of the person's condition. We need to exercise good judgement and be considerate to people's feelings especially when God reveals something which might be a little bit delicate. Remember Father's aim is to restore them, it is not to expose them. However, if you are certain of what God has shown you then proceed carefully. You may well have discovered the key that will unlock the situation. This requires discernment and sensitivity to the Spirit and to whoever you are ministering to!

- Always be careful when making **physical contact** with someone and always ask permission. You may say something along the lines of, "do you mind if I put my hand on your shoulder?" or "do you mind if I hold your hand?" Always use your common sense and never touch inappropriately. Be careful if you happen to be a demonstrative and tactile person, especially pertinent for the ladies among us! In church we greet each other with a 'holy kiss' but in the world people are not always comfortable with as much physical contact as perhaps we are accustomed to in the church. Please remember this and be sensitive. Even if the person being ministered to says it's 'OK', if they react to the contact, withdraw the hand.

Finally, it is always worth asking if the person would like to stay in contact and take their contact details so that you can continue to pray for them and get in touch to see how they are progressing. If they are uncomfortable with this, do not push the issue.

Before going your separate ways always ask them if they have any questions about anything that has taken place during the time of ministry. Talking with them will often reveal other areas in their lives where they would welcome some input. They might be receptive to being introduced to a Mother and Toddler group for example or a Seniors Coffee Morning at your church. It is a good idea to have a bit of a chat and possibly discover how you can maintain and foster further contact.

These are general guidelines for ministering. You may decide to fine tune them for your particular situation. Please do! I would suggest that they are a good foundation that can be built upon. We revisit these guidelines within our ministry on a regular basis. Both to remind ourselves of the advice and to make modifications as necessary. Of course, we should always rely on the leading of the Holy Spirit but we do that from a place of confidence in a set of principles we have put in place.

CHAPTER THIRTEEN

Personal Testimony of Healing

Stating the obvious, I know, but as you have read this book you will have picked up that one of the labels my husband bears is that of a 'healing evangelist'. Whereas such titles are not always helpful, in this instance it speaks to an anointing of God that Tim carries.

We have both sought to walk in the promise of Father that by Jesus' stripes we are healed and have tried to live out of the good of this truth throughout our life together. So, we are not ones for visiting doctors for every ailment, not that there is anything inherently amiss in consulting with the medical profession. We all have benefitted from their expertise at some point in our lives! Tim and I have just endeavoured to place our trust in God for our health over the years.

My story starts in January of 2016 when after feeling pretty miserable for several months, Tim packed me off to see the GP. I had spent the holiday in discomfort and was unable to enjoy the turkey dinner and all the lovely treats we associate with the

Christmas celebrations. The pain in my tummy was increasing and getting beyond a joke. My initial thought was that I was suffering from a bout of irritable bowel syndrome.

My doctor examined me and asked, "how did you get to the surgery? Is there anyone at home who can drive you?" Having assured her that my husband was at home she told me to go straight back and have Tim drive me to our local hospital as soon as possible. Within three hours I had been admitted to the Royal Surrey in Guildford, poked, prodded, tested, scanned and sent to a ward. After a further couple of hours five doctors trooped in to speak to us. You know that it is never going to be good news when they congregate around your bed with sombre expressions having closed the curtains! They broke the news that I was suffering from a rare form of incurable cancer.

To be honest, it was a surreal moment. My initial reaction was, "but I'm married to a healing evangelist! Nowhere in my belief system is there room for me to be this sick!"

Weeks followed of extensive testing and biopsies where they were trying to locate the primary tumour but they were unable to find it. The decision was made not to delay any longer and I underwent surgery in the May where they removed my gall bladder, appendix and as much of my liver as they dared without sending me into organ failure.

Thankfully, on searching through every inch of my gut they found a tumour in my small intestine and chopped it out.

That little tumour was the culprit and had probably been there for years busily sending out little storm troopers of disease that had marched through my lymph system like an invading army leaving outposts of disease as it went.

This particular cancer is a sneaky disease. By the time you have symptoms, for me pain when I ate, it has metastasized, it has spread, and you are in trouble.

An expected three to five day stay in hospital turned into an eighteen day marathon, much of it spent in the Intensive Care Unit as my system went on strike. There was a constant struggle to find an effective level of pain control which made for some fairly grim times.

On meeting with the surgeon he informed us that the operation had not gone as well as they had hoped and that the scans prior to the procedure had not prepared them for the extent of the cancer. He explained that my remaining liver was riddled with pin prick tumours which they could do nothing about surgically and a transplant was not an option. He was handing me back to the tender care of the oncology department.

We talked prognosis with the doctor there and his response was, "we try to turn days into weeks, weeks into months and months into years". OKaaay, I thought. When we pushed him as to where we sat on that time scale, he paused and then said, "well, we will try and get you through to the end of the year". That was in the May. So six, seven months.

We told our children but determined to keep that piece of the jigsaw to ourselves. Our personal faith challenge. Tim and I decided that our confession for the last forty years of our marriage would not change. 'God is faithful'. So we daily spoke words of faith into the situation.

Father pointed me to a couple of Scriptures. Psalm 118:17 says, *'I shall not die but shall live to declare the praises of the Lord'* and *'He is reliable, trustworthy and faithful and ever true to His promise and He **can** be depended on'* (1 Corinthians 1:9 AMP).

So we stated that my body is a cancer free zone regardless of what the scans were showing. That was our position of faith and we declared it daily.

I made these verses my own. I determined as best as I could to get hold of the Word of God and let the Word of God get a hold of me.

The medical profession were quite clear with us; they cannot cure this condition. The best that they can do is to slow the growth of the tumours which were throughout my liver, in my abdomen, near to my heart and in my neck. Their aim is to control the symptoms and improve quality of life. To give you longer basically.

Guildford said that such was the 'volume of disease' that they would refer us straight away to Guys in London to see if they would include me in a research programme funded outside of the NHS. This would involve radio-nuclide therapy to try to slow the progress of the disease. The Professor reviewed my case and we were accepted into her care.

It was our great joy to see our daughter married in the summer of 2017 when there had been a very real doubt during the dark moments, in my mind at least, that I would make it that far.

Having been referred to Guys we attended every few months for scans. Just before the Christmas of 2017 the Professor told us that there was 'some movement' in the various trouble spots and she felt that it would be best to undergo the treatment that they offered starting in the New Year.

That was disappointing news. The monthly hormone injections were no longer holding the disease at bay. But we continued to speak it out; 'God is faithful to His Word… I shall not die but live'.

The therapy consisted of four treatments spread over the course of approximately a year. Each included a battery of tests and an overnight stay in isolation. After each round, once your bone marrow starts to recover, they zap you again! The nausea was manageable but the fatigue was crushing and I spent weeks resting up after each round.

With each visit, the doctors reminded us that the treatment is not curative. It is a palliative measure aimed at arresting the growth of the tumours and bettering your quality of life. When we attended for the second round, the doctor reviewed the latest scan with us. He remarked, "this is very unusual. We never see any change in cancer size this early on in the regime. The tumour in your neck has disappeared!"

We received this news as a 'first fruit' of all that Father was going to do.

Our confession continued to be that 'I am a cancer free zone' and that although we are so very grateful for all that the doctors can do (God bless our healthcare system!) we believed that the Holy Spirit would continue to work beyond where the medicine finishes.

I underwent the final treatment at the end of 2018. We saw the Professor to discuss the scans taken that day compared with the previous three sets. She asked me what I could see. I tentatively ventured, "I can't see anything there". She replied, "I know. This is an exceptional, exceptional result. I can see no appreciable cancer".

God is faithful.

She gave various caveats; "perhaps the scanner is malfunctioning, but I don't think so. I think this is genuine".

We returned to Guys a few weeks later at the beginning of the New Year for a whole battery of targeted scans and tests to confirm their findings. They found a couple of very small lesions in my liver and abdomen but we are confident that they too will disappear.

God has done far beyond what man can do. The Professor's

words were, "well, you really are not a typical patient". I have regular blood work to check various areas such as my liver function and will have scans every six months to monitor the condition.

I am so grateful to the NHS for their care and a big shout out for Macmillan who were wonderful in helping with the long recovery from the surgery. I continue to look to Father to achieve more than the medics are able to deliver. He is our ultimate Healer!

Then came the challenge of weaning myself off of the oxycodone. Morphine and these other opioids are wonderful stuff until you have to kick the habit! I am now free.

In October of 2019 I returned to Guys for another barrage of scans and tests. On meeting with the consultant, he said, "These are astounding results! Quite outstanding. I am discharging you from Guys Cancer Clinic, there's no point in you coming back here".

I am not a 'typical patient'. I am humbled by Father's continued mercy on my life.

It is in that place of challenge that I have had the opportunity to see the fullness of God's glory revealed as we have spoken words of faith over my life. Undeniably, there have been some dark times and, indeed, some very scary days. My Father God is faithful to His Word and I can rest safe in His arms as He continues to work His miracle of healing in my body by the power of the Holy Spirit.

I am no longer held hostage by cancer. *'I shall not die but will live to speak out the praises of the Lord'*.

I would encourage each and every one of you to continue to look to God for your miracle even when you think rationally it could never happen. Father is in the business of doing *'infinitely more than all we ask or imagine according to His power that is at work within us'* (Ephesians 3:20). Whatever area of your life needs a touch from Him, be it your health, finances, relationships or future hopes and ambitions. Our Almighty Father is ever faithful to His Word because, above all else, we can be secure in the fact that He loves us beyond measure.

Kim Grant

March 2021

Recommended by the Author

Living Without A Safety Net
Tim Grant
ISBN 978-1-911086-35-2

Packed with remarkable accounts of healings, miracles and salvation, it tells how Tim encountered Jesus in his early life and how he began to walk by faith and bring Christ's love to countless lives. In each of Tim's stories there is a pearl of wisdom to be found – a lesson he learned about the walk of faith, often with far-reaching effects. As you read these testimonies you will find yourself hungry to see God move in the same way in your own family, neighbourhood and church; you will be challenged to simply step out, trust and obey.

Living A Kingdom Prophetic Lifestyle
Chris Larkin
ISBN978-1-905991-02-0

'Filled with practical insights, wisdom and revelation, this is a great development tool for individuals and small groups. If you can't get Chris into your church or your region, get the book! You won't be the same again!' *GRAHAM COOKE.* 'What a delight it is at long last to have a book that, in a simple way, explains and deals with the issues of the King and His kingdom and how we handle and interpret prophecy. This book should have a wide readership because it will help many who are on the journey of discovering their destiny in God.' *NORMAN BARNES, Founder, Links International Missions Network.*